W9-BMM-542

Laura Stamm's Power Skating

third edition

Laura Stamm

The Laura Stamm International Power Skating System

Human Kinetics

Library of Congress Cataloging-in-Publication Data

Stamm, Laura.
   [Power skating]
   Laura Stamm's power skating / Laura Stamm.--3rd ed.
     p. cm.
   Includes bibliographical references (p.).
   ISBN 0-7360-3735-7
    1. Hockey--Training. 2. Skating. I. Title.

   GV848.3 .S7 2001
   796.962'2--dc21   2001024792

ISBN: **0-7360-3735-7**

Copyright © 2001, 1989, 1982 by Laura Stamm

All rights reserved. Except for use in a review, the reproduction or utilization of this work in any form or by any electronic, mechanical, or other means, now known or hereafter invented, including xerography, photocopying, and recording, and in any information storage and retrieval system, is forbidden without the written permission of the publisher.

Production Editor: Melinda Graham; **Assistant Editors:** Scott Hawkins, John Wentworth; **Copyeditor:** Jackie Blakley; **Proofreader:** Sarah Wiseman; **Graphic Designer:** Nancy Rasmus; **Graphic Artist:** Dody Bullerman; **Photo Manager:** Clark Brooks; **Cover Designer:** Keith Blomberg; **Photographer (cover):** © Doug Trojanowski, American I Photo, Inc.; **Photographers (interior):** Bruce Bennett, Erik Hill, Jerry Liebman; page 17, © Layne Murdoch, SportsChrome USA; pages 90, 153, and 184 © Gregg Forwerck, SportsChrome USA; page 206, Rob Skeoch, The Picture Desk; **Art Manager:** Craig Newsom; **Illustrators:** Accurate Art, Inc., Tim Offenstein; **Printer:** Bang Printing

Human Kinetics books are available at special discounts for bulk purchase. Special editions or book excerpts can also be created to specification. For details, contact the Special Sales Manager at Human Kinetics.

Printed in the United States of America
10 9 8 7 6 5 4 3 2 1

Human Kinetics
Web site: www.humankinetics.com

United States: Human Kinetics
P.O. Box 5076
Champaign, IL 61825-5076
800-747-4457
e-mail: humank@hkusa.com

Canada: Human Kinetics
475 Devonshire Road Unit 100
Windsor, ON N8Y 2L5
800-465-7301 (in Canada only)
e-mail: orders@hkcanada.com

Europe: Human Kinetics
Units C2/C3 Wira Business Park
West Park Ring Road
Leeds LS16 6EB, United Kingdom
+44 (0) 113 278 1708
e-mail: hk@hkeurope.com

Australia: Human Kinetics
57A Price Avenue
Lower Mitcham, South Australia 5062
08 8277 1555
e-mail: liahka@senet.com.au

New Zealand: Human Kinetics
P.O. Box 105-231, Auckland Central
09-523-3462
e-mail: hkp@ihug.co.nz

To my beloved family—always and still the inspiration and cornerstone of my life. But especially to my mother, by whose example I learned to reach for the sky.

To my extended family—all the hockey players, big and small, pro and peewee, whom I have known over these 30 years.

To all those who have believed in me—you helped fulfill dreams beyond imagination.

The sport of hockey has enriched my life beyond measure; there is nothing else I could have done in life with such passion and such dedication.

To those whose lives I have touched in the teaching process, please know that you have touched my life in return.

Just as I learned that there is no difference between teaching and learning, I also learned that there is no difference between giving and receiving.

contents

foreword

The legendary Anatoli Tarasov once said, "You will not get far using old skates, using old tactics, skill, and techniques." That statement was true when he coached his Soviet teams to nine world championships, and it is especially true in today's fast-paced game. Superior skating is essential for success to players and teams.

Fortunately, skating is a skill that can be developed through proper training and technique. NHL stars weren't born with their amazing skating ability; they mastered the fundamentals, then worked many hours to refine their movements and to become more powerful on skates. In many cases they've benefitted from the lessons of an expert skating instructor, providing them special insights and tips to gain that split-second advantage over the competition.

In this book, Laura Stamm offers you the same, special technical advice and drills that have made her such a popular skating instructor. If you believe you can skate better, she will show you how. I highly recommend this book to all players and coaches.

Herb Brooks
Coach, 2002 U.S. Olympic Men's Ice Hockey Team
Coach, 1980 U.S. Gold Medal Olympic Team
Member of U.S. and International Hockey Hall of Fame

preface

I have loved skating for as long as I can remember. There's something about the feeling of freedom on ice, of not being bound by gravity—something about the speed, flow, sheer beauty of the skating motion. For me, skating has been a life-long passion.

When I was growing up, there was no organized hockey for girls, but I played on the ponds with my brothers and friends. When I became a competitive figure skater, I would spend hours watching the New York Rangers go through their practices. At that time wingers skated up and down the wings. Centers skated up and down the center. Defensemen hung back in the defensive zone.

I started asking some of the Ranger players questions such as, "Why don't you all circle and weave like Bobby Orr? Why don't you 'give and go' like they do in basketball?" The players, amused, asked me, "Why don't you mind your own business?" Then they asked me if I'd like to teach "power skating" at their summer hockey school. I jumped at the chance, never realizing that this was to be the start of something big.

Very little was known or understood at that time (1971) about the science (biomechanics) of hockey skating. My first day at the hockey school I was handed a sheet of paper that had the words POWER SKATING written at the top and listed specific drills underneath. The drills included stops and starts, skate to the blue line and back, skate forward, turn around, skate backward and hurry on back to the starting point, skate the circles, etc. This appeared to be the sum total of power skating. Not a word was mentioned about teaching players how to skate correctly. And I had no one to ask.

I went on the ice that day with three groups of boys. The groups were divided by age; the youngest student was about eight, the oldest about eighteen. Nick Fotiu, future NHLer, was one of these. I watched, stunned, as these guys raced around the ice, going nowhere fast, legs churning ineffectively. Coaches at that time knew very little about skating technique, and of course the players knew even less. From the first minute, it was apparent to me that these young hockey players needed to learn *how* to skate correctly!

I "stashed" the sheet of paper and started experimenting with a brain full of ideas. Four books, two videos, several thousands of amateur and pro students, 30 years later, and I'm still at it—still learning, still experimenting, still believing that the most important aspect of a player's training is to develop correct hockey skating techniques.

I didn't know it then, but I was teaching the "European" method of skating, without ever having seen European hockey. I believed that players must learn to utilize full, powerful, and explosive strides, and combine these with mobility and control. When I got to watch the Soviets play against the NHL, I knew I was on the right track.

Without knowing it or seeking to, I jump-started the careers of hundreds, maybe thousands, of pro players; spawned the development of an entire industry, and was the model for (and often the teacher of) a new generation of power skating hockey instructors who followed in my footsteps.

Hockey skating has come a long way in these 30 years. We now have sophisticated methods to measure speed, acceleration, body angles, edge angles, knee bend, etc. Players now circle and weave, give and go. Defenders rush as if they were forwards, forwards play back to cover for the rushing defenders. The game is faster every year. Players are bigger, stronger, faster and highly skilled. Girls and women are playing the sport and getting better every year. Players who can't keep up have little chance of making it at the highest levels. Every hockey school, almost every rink, offers some form of power skating instruction. I'm teaching my second, even third-generation of players—the children and grandchildren of former students who seek me out to teach their young ones.

The 2001 All Star Event featured a skating competition won by Billy Guerin. He was clocked at 29 mph. This would have been unheard of 30 years ago. I wonder how fast the game will be 30 years from now?

The sport has come a long way, and as the skill level continues to increase hockey will become even more exciting. I feel very fortunate to have been there early on, to have catalyzed its development, and in the process, influenced so many lives.

acknowledgments

This book may have just one author but it could not be written without the help of many. I express deep thanks and gratitude to all those who helped me make it a reality:

NHL player Doug Brown, and pro player Greg Brown, for their fabulous skating and unending support.

The other hockey players who gave their time, energy and skating. Mark Pecchia, Louis Santini, Richard Stamm and Gordon Campbell.

Herb Brooks, with whom I had the honor of working when he coached the New York Rangers and from whom I learned so much.

Marshall Rule, for his expertise, knowledge, and lifelong friendship. He has always been my mentor. Our intellectual battles continue to further my education in skating.

Bruce Bennett, Erik Hill and Jerry Liebman for their excellent photography.

Melinda Graham, my editor at Human Kinetics Publishers, who worked endlessly to produce a book far better than would have been possible had I been deprived of her dedication and meticulous attention to detail.

Julia Duncan and Ben Wilks, who with their youthful insight contributed some great ideas.

introduction

Coaches' Corner

All hockey coaches want their players to reach their full potential. But even coaches who are knowledgeable about offensive, defensive, and strategic aspects of the game often are not well versed in the science of power skating.

Skating is not the most exciting aspect of hockey. Kids want to play the game, not practice skating. The challenge for a coach or power skating instructor is to teach the skating mechanics so they are well understood, and at the same time make learning challenging and fun. Once players realize that their hockey is improving because their skating is improving, they become willing students. As they get more ice time, become able to play on the power play or when the team is shorthanded, they make the connection between skating ability and ice time.

People learn in many different ways. Some learn visually, some learn by imitating, others learn by feeling, and yet others learn as a result of understanding. No single method works for everyone. Usually the learning process requires a combination of these methods. Experiment to find what works and what doesn't. Change explanations and illustrations accordingly. Some students do better when left on their own to work out ideas. Others need gentle prodding. Some need downright insistence. All need praise and encouragement.

I have found that teaching by saying "Follow me" or "Do this" doesn't work. People see things differently. While they think they are "doing this," they may actually be doing something quite different. I have also discovered that asking "Do you understand?" is not an effective way to gauge students' understanding. Very few players have the courage to admit that they don't understand; instead, they act as if they do, then perform incorrectly. Ask them to explain what you mean, then ask them to show you what they mean. Accept mistakes as a natural part of learning. Most of all, let them know you care!

My teaching system is based on the fact that skating is not a natural motion. It is, in fact, one of the most unnatural motions an athlete may execute. I've seen too many players skate laboriously when stickhandling down the ice because they haven't learned to skate FAST with the puck.

The principles of skating FAST are as follows:

Feel what you're doing (sensory)

Act out what you feel (perform)

See in your mind's eye how the move is done (visualize)

Think about and analyze the move (intellectual)

Feel, Act, See, Think = FAST

Sound is another helpful learning tool. Sounds that the blades make on the ice differ for every maneuver, and they differ when done correctly as compared to when done incorrectly. Teach students to listen to distinguish between correct and incorrect execution.

Tips for Coaches of Youth Players

Youngsters need to have fun—and coaches need to remember this!

1. We are teachers and should approach coaching with that in mind. Our job is to stimulate in young people an enjoyment of learning, inquisitiveness, creativity, and love for the sport.

2. Learn from watching the best. Study great NHL skaters. Videotape their skating maneuvers; watch these in slow motion so you can pass along what you observe to your students.

3. Reward is more effective than punishment. I recently watched Larry Robinson, coach of the 2000 Stanley Cup champion New Jersey Devils, put his arm around the shoulder of a player who had just come off the ice after a tough shift. This coach knew when to lay down the law, but he also knew when to build up his players. I thought to myself, *This player will give his heart and soul for this coach because he is treated with respect.* Tough love has its place in hockey, as it does in life.

4. Build self-esteem. Encourage respect for teammates, opponents, coaches, referees, and observers. Teach life lessons. Teach sportsmanship and fair play, how to win and lose with grace.

5. Although each player's skating style is unique, certain skating principles are universal and must be adhered to. It is the coach's job to teach and reinforce these principles. It takes many years to become a finished skater, so don't expect instant success.

6. Youngsters get restless easily, so keep them skating as much as possible. Organize the ice with this in mind. Skate the entire length of ice when the group is small, but skate from sideboards to sideboards when the group is large. Use small group stations when applicable. Sense when the group is becoming restless and change the activity before you "lose" it.

7. Have players practice each technique slowly at first. The brain needs time to absorb complicated information and transfer it to the muscles. The muscles, after receiving the information, will then struggle to make the necessary changes. Players must understand that correct practice and repetition are essential if the changes are to become permanent.

8. Use controlled scrimmages or games with skating technique as the focus. Specific skating maneuvers can be practiced in these scrimmages by establishing rules such as the following:

- Player with the puck must do two or three crossovers before shooting.
- Player with the puck must pivot or turn around (forward to backward or backward to forward) or spin around 360 degrees, before shooting.
- Player with the puck must do two or three stops and starts, or transition from slow to fast, before shooting.
- Player with the puck must make a certain number of lateral maneuvers before shooting.
- Players must skate as a team and practice "give and go" two or three times before shooting.
- Player with the puck must go around an obstacle course of other players before shooting.

9. Use prizes and races to stimulate the competitive spirit. My feeling, however, is that races are helpful once skills have been developed, but can be detrimental when skills are just being learned. Players caught in the frenzy of trying to win will neglect technique.

10. When possible, explain your goals for the day before going on the ice. Players will then be ready to work when they hit the ice. Since ice time has a way of flying by, it's important to establish an effective talk–skating ratio. Alternate soundbite explanations with longer periods of skating. But don't allow players to skate sloppily. Make them concentrate on skating correctly. Stop them if the skating disintegrates into sloppiness. Let them know your goal is to take them out of their comfort zone.

11. Praise, patience, and encouragement are key. Treat players with dignity. Respect begets respect. Coaches do not have to rule by intimidation, and they should not.

12. Mistakes are not high crimes. Youngsters fear looking bad and will refuse to experiment for fear of embarrassment, criticism, or reprimand. Keep reminding them that everyone falls, even the pros and that mistakes are inevitable and often an indication that the player is trying something new. Not only should you accept mistakes, you should acknowledge a good try even when a player wipes out. The improvement that occurs once players no

longer fear criticism is amazing to behold. Perhaps you should even take a dive yourself once in a while to show that nobody, not even the teacher, is perfect.

13. Rely on players who take learning seriously. More often than not, they turn out to be your most reliable performers.

Format of the Book

Each chapter of this book is divided into three sections. The first section includes a detailed explanation of the skating maneuver being discussed. The second section includes drills and exercises to practice that maneuver. The exercises progress from the simplest to the most difficult. All exercises should be practiced first without the puck, then with the puck. The third section is a brief summary of the chapter.

Combining the Exercises

The exercises in this book can be combined. For example,

1. Combine turn exercises with knee-drop exercises.
2. Combine crossover exercises with pivots.
3. Use obstacle courses.
4. Use a stopwatch to time players.

Points to Remember

- Develop a philosophy of teaching and adhere to it.
- Affection and discipline are not mutually exclusive.
- Teaching can sometimes be like pulling teeth, but insistence on high standards pays off. Whenever possible, learning should be fun, but sometimes players must be made to learn in spite of themselves.
- Inventiveness, creativity, and analytic thinking should be valued and encouraged. Screaming coaches only stifle creativity. Wayne Gretzky was not the product of intimidation but was given the freedom to Feel, Act, See, and Think (FAST) and make mistakes along the way.

chapter 1

Skates and Equipment for Superior Skating

You wouldn't start a trip without a map and some plans. In the same way, you shouldn't start skating until you've considered and followed these suggestions. One of the most important aspects of hockey is protective equipment. When performing the exercises in this book, always wear full protective hockey equipment: helmet, face mask or shield, mouthpiece, neck guard, shoulder and chest pads, elbow pads, pants, shin guards, and gloves. Keep the helmet chin strap securely fastened at all times. In a fall, you need to rely on the helmet to protect you from a head injury!

Because skating exercises require experimentation, falls are inevitable and should be considered as normal as breathing. By wearing protective equipment when practicing, you lower the risk of injury and also become accustomed to skating at your game weight.

Your skates are your most important equipment. The quality, fit, manner of lacing, sharpening, and maintenance of your skates all affect performance. Therefore, an inexpensive model of skates is a bad investment, and buying boots big enough for a youngster to wear for a few years is penny-wise and pound-foolish. To skate well, skaters must have well-constructed boots that fit properly and blades made of well-tempered steel that are sharpened properly.

Buying and Fitting Skate Boots

Boots that are well constructed and fit properly enhance performance. The function of the skate boots is to support the feet firmly, while still allowing skaters to lean their boots inward and outward, which is necessary for executing difficult and intricate maneuvers. Good boots have reinforcing material in the counter (instep) area. The reinforcing material makes that area of the boots especially supportive for the arches and ankles. If boots are well made, you should not be able to squeeze the counter and ankle areas together.

Unless there has been a specific injury to the foot, weak ankles are generally a myth. If ankles cave in, the cause is usually boots that are ill-fitting or have poorly constructed counters. Lack of ankle support almost guarantees that correct skating will be difficult and even uncomfortable. Ankles that cave in cause pain!

Several companies specialize in manufacturing skates and hockey equipment. All offer several models of hockey skates, ranging from very inexpensive to exorbitantly expensive. Boots may be made of leather, molded plastic, nylon, or a combination of these. Top-of-the-line boots fit better, provide more support, last longer, and offer better protection against injury from pucks or sticks. Choose your skates wisely—they are instrumental in preparing you to develop the skating skills necessary for speed, agility, and power.

Follow these guidelines for selecting skates:

1. Boots should fit like a glove—snug but comfortable—and should hug the feet firmly. The toes should come right up to the front of the boot, yet should not be pinched or curled up on one another. They should fit most snugly at the instep and across the ball of the foot. If you can move your feet sideways within the boots, they are too wide. If you can lift your heels when you lean forward, the boots are too long.

2. When being fitted for new boots, wear the same weight of sock you will wear when skating. A sock of different weight can change the fit. A thin sock is best so that the boots can mold themselves to your feet as they get broken in. Once broken in, boots should feel as though they are a natural part of your feet. I do not advise wearing thick socks or two pairs of socks, as this acts to "disconnect" your feet from the boots.

A note for players who wear corrective orthotics—it's fine to wear them in your skates, and they will improve your balance and performance. But remember that the size of the boots must accommodate the orthotics, so it's important to bring them along when being fitted for new skates.

3. Before putting your feet into the boots, unlace them most of the way. Trying to jam your foot into a boot that is three-quarters laced is an exercise in frustration—your feet just won't go in, and you'll think the boots are too small.

4. To test the width of the boots, lace them snugly. There should be a spread of 1½ to 2 inches between the eyelets on the same row. If the laces are closer together than this, the boots are too wide for your feet; your ankles will cave inward when skating. If your heels slip or you can lift them, the boots are too long.

5. Each manufacturer builds boots on a different mold, so while one brand might fit well, another might be uncomfortable. Also, skate boot sizes usually differ from street shoe sizes.

6. It's best to be fitted for skates at a shop that specializes in hockey skates and equipment. The employees are often knowledgeable about all brands and models, and can help you purchase the skates that best meet your needs.

7. Today's skates tend to be extremely stiff and difficult to break in. Players who wear them for hours at a time and on a daily basis prefer stiff boots because they last longer. But youngsters, small adults, females, and recre-

ational players have an especially difficult time breaking them in. For these players I recommend buying a brand or model that is a bit less stiff. Another option is to buy a good pair of secondhand skates. Youngsters outgrow their skates long before breaking them down, maybe even before breaking them in. It's far better to buy good-quality used skates than poor-quality new skates.

Note: If purchasing used skates, be sure the blades are in good condition and not sharpened down excessively. Many shops carry used skates, and many hockey groups hold annual skate swaps (usually at the beginning of the hockey season).

Lacing the Skates

Although at first it may not seem critical, proper lacing of one's skates is essential to good performance. Many skaters tighten their laces excessively. This limits foot mobility and cuts off circulation, which in turn causes numbness and cramps in the feet. Boots should support the feet, not immobilize them. Properly laced skates will support your feet while still allowing you to bend your knees readily and roll your ankles and boots inward and outward without restriction. Too often I encounter players who cannot bend their knees or roll their ankles adequately because they are in a vise. Lace bite is a common injury caused by excessively tight laces.

The tightest area of lacing should be from a point above the ball of the foot back to a point just above the ankle (see figure 1.1). This is where the most support is required. The toe area (front) and the area high above the ankles should be moderately snug. Some elite players prefer the area above the ankle a bit loose; some even choose not to lace the very top set of eyelets. This is a personal choice for them, but young and developing players should lace all the sets of eyelets.

Do not wrap tape around your ankles. This inhibits foot mobility and is unnecessary.

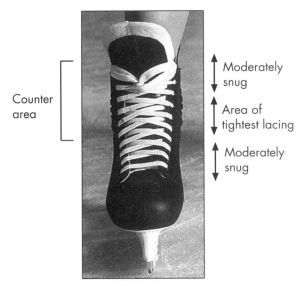

Figure 1.1 Correct lacing of the boot.

Coaching Tip

If laces are too tight at the top, bending your knees and ankles becomes difficult and uncomfortable. Snug is good; pain is not!

I recommend that players place their shin pads *inside* the tongues of the boots rather than *over* the tongues. This allows for more freedom to bend the knees. Just be sure the shin pads are long enough to come all the way down your leg. You don't want an area where a puck could find an unprotected spot.

Tips for Breaking in New Boots

- Lace the boots quite loosely during the breaking-in process.
- Wear new skates at home; put the skate guards on and walk around in them for 30 to 60 minutes at a time.
- Some players like to put on their socks, wet their feet, then put the skates on and walk around in them. Water acts like sweat; it is sweat that eventually breaks in the boots.
- Never wear new skates for an important skating or hockey event. Break them in first, during practices or at open skating sessions. It's common to get blisters during the breaking-in process. This is one of the unfortunate realities that all players must deal with. We all hate breaking in new skates!
- Some players wear their new skates for short periods on the ice and go back to wearing their old ones for the rest of the session. The hope is to limit the uncomfortable breaking-in time and also to avoid blisters.
- If you feel a blister starting, take off the new boots or try inserting a "second skin" material on the affected area. You can also cut a hole in a foam sponge to make a "doughnut" and place this over the affected area; this will eliminate contact and pressure between the boot and that part of your foot.

The Skate Blades

Quality hockey skates have blades of high-quality, heat-tempered steel that retain a sharp edge despite extremely rough use. The blades are only to be used on the ice. Wear skate guards, even when walking on the rubber mats in rink hallways and locker rooms. Never expose the blades to cement, steel, concrete, or wood surfaces, because they will get nicked and dulled. Inexpensive blades nick and dull easily and have to be sharpened frequently. Most high-quality boots also have high-quality blades, but there are several brands of blades. Players can buy their favorite blades and have them mounted on their boots. Regardless of the brand, new blades *must* be sharpened before skating on them!

Blades rust easily. After getting off the ice, dry them thoroughly with a towel and put terrycloth skate guards on them. When you get home, take the guards off and air-dry the blades. Now put *dry* terrycloth guards back on the blades and put the skates back in your hockey bag. Never store blades in rubber skate guards; they retain moisture and the blades will rust. When you're away from skating for long periods, store your skates without any guards on, in a dry environment. You don't want to be that unlucky player who, at the beginning of a new season, goes to the rink, takes the skates out of the hockey bag, and finds they're totally covered with rust. No skating that day!

Blade Design

Each skate blade, from toe to heel, is designed with two knifelike edges that are separated by a groove. The function of the groove is to expose the edges, enabling them to cut into the ice more effectively. This groove is called the *hollow* (figure 1.2). The blade can be sharpened so that the hollow is either shallow or deep, depending on the player's preference. In general, a deep hollow makes it difficult to execute a smooth, effective stop because the edges can unexpectedly dig into the ice. Too shallow a hollow can make it difficult to execute sharp turns and powerful pushes.

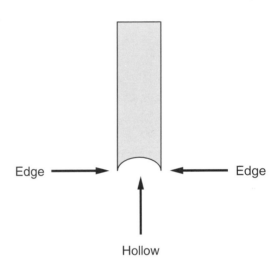

Figure 1.2 Cross section of the blade, showing the edges and the hollow.

Small children (with little body weight) require sharper blades and a relatively deep hollow to enable the edges to dig into the ice more easily. Conversely, heavier people can skate with less sharp blades and a shallower hollow.

The shape of the hockey skate blade is convex (curved). This curved shape is called the *rock*, or *radius,* and resembles a crescent moon or the legs of a rocking chair (figure 1.3). The rock of the blade makes it possible for skaters to maneuver in tight curves and circles. If the blades were straight like those of speed skates, hockey players could gain speed when skating straight ahead, but it would be difficult to weave, cut, or execute sharp turns.

Because they need to move in a straight line forward, backward, or sideways rather than perform weaving or circular maneuvers, goalies use blades that are almost straight rather than convex. Curved blades also would hinder their ability to make skate saves. Goaltenders don't sharpen their

Figure 1.3 Hockey blade, showing the rock.

skates as often as other players do; they need blades dull enough to enable them to slide sideways across the goal crease.

If a blade is sharpened and *rockered* (curved) to an extreme degree, very little blade length makes contact with the ice. Sharply rockered blades are popular with some pros, but many prefer to have more blade length and a shallow hollow. Sharply rockered blades can make balancing difficult, and having so little blade length in contact with the ice restricts power and speed.

Sharpening the Blades

Blades should be kept sharp and free from nicks and dents. Dull, nicked blades do not grip the ice effectively; the result is a loss of power, speed, and maneuverability. Dull blades can unexpectedly slip out from under the skater. If this happens during a sudden move, it can cause falls and painful muscle pulls or tears.

Blades should be sharpened when they no longer dig crisply into the ice. They should be sharpened by an expert. Some professional hockey players sharpen their skates after every game; some even sharpen them after each period. However, this isn't necessary or even desirable for most nonprofessional players, as excessive sharpening shortens the life of the blades.

How to Test the Sharpening

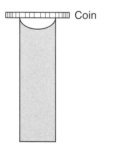

Figure 1.4 Blade cross section, showing level, properly sharpened edges.

If the blade is properly sharpened, the inside and outside edges are level with each other. To test the accuracy of the sharpening, place a coin horizontally on the upturned blade. Study the angle of the coin. If it is perfectly level, the edges are even (figure 1.4). If the coin tilts to either side, they are not. Take the skates back for resharpening; if one edge is higher than the other, your skating will be impaired.

Blades can become increasingly rockered if the sharpener is not careful. Ultimately, too little blade will be in contact with the ice. Tell the sharpener precisely how sharp you want your skates to be, how much hollow and rocker you want, and where you want the high point of the rocker to be. Some players make and keep a template of their blades. To do this, trace an outline of the blades after the first couple of sharpenings. After each successive sharpening, measure the blades against the template and make sure that they conform to it. Also, ask the sharpener to hand stone the blades after each sharpening. This will guarantee smooth, finished edges.

Note: Forwards generally prefer the high point of the rocker to be just behind the middle of the blade; defenders prefer that it be just in front of the middle of the blade.

The Edges

Every skate blade has two edges. The edges toward the insides of the boots are called the *inside edges* (figure 1.5a), and those toward the outsides of the boots are called the *outside edges* (figure 1.5b). The edges have a specific purpose: to cut into the ice. In doing this they perform two completely different and separate functions. One is to create motion (the power or pushing edge); the other is to establish direction (the edge that glides on a curved path). Understanding how the edges function and how best to use them is key to all movement on ice.

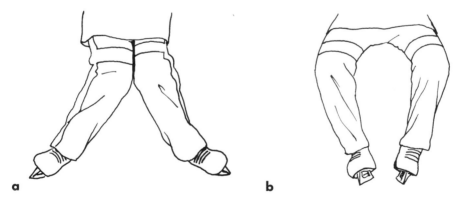

a   b

Figure 1.5 *(a)* Inside and *(b)* outside edges.

Pushing

When used for pushing, the edges of the blades must dig into the ice to provide the grip against which the pushing leg thrusts for movement (power). If you push without first digging the edge into the ice, the skate will slip. You might attribute this to the ice being slippery, but the ice should *never* feel slippery. If you use the edges properly, they should be able to grip the ice strongly. Try to *feel* the edges cut into the ice. Even when gliding straight ahead on two feet, skaters incline slightly toward the inside edges for balance and stability.

Gliding

When used for gliding, the edges establish the direction of travel. Because blades are rockered, edges glide a curved path. When gliding on the left forward inside edge (LFI), you travel in a clockwise direction. When gliding on the right forward inside edge (RFI), you travel in a counterclockwise direction. When gliding on the left forward outside edge (LFO), you travel in a counterclockwise direction; and when gliding on the right forward outside edge (RFO), you travel in a clockwise direction.

Going backward, the directions are reversed. When gliding on the left backward inside edge (LBI): counterclockwise. Gliding on the right backward inside edge (RBI): clockwise. Gliding on the left backward outside edge (LBO): clockwise. Gliding on the right backward outside edge (RBO): counterclockwise.

Glide direction	Edge
Clockwise	LFI, RFO, RBI, LBO
Counterclockwise	RFI, LFO, LBI, RBO

How the Skates and Body Coordinate to Produce Curves

A common misconception in hockey is that the skates should always be held straight up. When skates are held straight up, you ride simultaneously on the inside and outside edges (the flats) of the blades. Since the flat of each blade describes a straight line on the ice, you will travel either straight forward or straight backward. But you can neither glide on a curve nor grip the ice with the flat of the blade. You must use the edges—both for pushing and for traveling a curved path.

To get an edge to cut into the ice, lean the engaged boot so that the desired edge forms a sharp angle with the ice. To do this, press the engaged foot (the pushing or gliding foot) onto its side—it can be either the outside or the inside—and bend that knee in the same direction. Two important points:

1. When the thrusting (pushing) skate is on an edge, the more the foot presses, the boot leans, and the knee bends, the more the skate will grip the ice and the greater the potential for thrust against the ice. An edge that digs into the ice at an angle of 45 degrees (when traveling fast) is the optimum cutting edge (figure 1.6).

Figure 1.6 Thrusting foot on a strong inside edge; 90-degree knee bend.

2. When the gliding (skating) foot is on an edge, the more the foot presses, the boot leans, and the knee bends, the sharper will be your curve or circle. Try to achieve a knee bend of 90 degrees as measured between the thigh and shin of the gliding leg.

The skate alone cannot achieve the edge. The entire body coordinates to produce an effective pushing or gliding edge. To apply an inside edge, lean the boot, knee, and thigh toward the inside of your body (figure 1.7a). To apply an outside edge, lean the boot, knee, and thigh toward the outside of your body (figure 1.7b). The angle of your knee and thigh must line up above the skate so that all describe the same angle to the ice. The rest of your body weight (hips, torso, shoulders) is balanced over the engaged foot and presses downward toward the ice to assist the edge in gripping the ice. If your body weight is not totally over the engaged foot, or if it does not press downward sufficiently, the edge will grip less effectively, the curve will be shallow, and balance will be impaired.

a   **b**

Figure 1.7   *(a)* Gliding forward on inside edge (left foot); *(b)* gliding forward on outside edge (left foot).

When skating on a curve or circle, remember the following:

1. The faster you skate, the deeper the edge you must apply to the ice, and the more you need to bend your knees and press your body weight downward above the engaged edge.

2. Centripetal and centrifugal forces are at work; they must be equalized and in proportion to your speed in order for you to balance over the edge.

3. The skate blade travels as if it were on the outside rim of a circle. The body rides slightly inside the rim. The lower body (skating foot,

knee, thigh, and hips) presses toward the center of the circle, hips always facing the line of travel. The upper body (chest and shoulders) rests above the hips but still within the rim of the circle. If the upper body presses into the circle more than the lower body does, stability is jeopardized.

4. Figure 1.8 shows the body position essential to effective movement on a curve. Expert hockey players frequently employ this position for difficult maneuvers such as tight turns, crossovers, or pivots.

Figure 1.8 Body position for skating a curve.

Coaches often tell skaters to lean into the circle to obtain their curve. However, this advice often leads to the misconception that the upper body should be tilted into the circle. Only the lower body (skate, knee, thigh, and hips) leans into the circle. The upper body should be essentially upright (it does not lean), with shoulders level with the ice. Correct body positioning is one of the most important aspects of balance and must be mastered if you are to become a good hockey skater.

chapter 2

Balance for Stability and Speed

Great hockey players are so perfectly balanced that they appear to be linked to the ice by a magnetic force. It's common to take balance for granted and overlook its importance, but it is one of the most important aspects of hockey. Achieving balance is critical for all players; mastering it will enable you to skate with greater maneuverability and speed, perform high-velocity turns, execute sudden starts and stops, change direction more quickly, shoot more powerfully, and deliver and withstand crunching body checks.

Many different balance situations exist in hockey, and all should be mastered. Some players can balance well on two skates but not on one. Some can balance on one skate on the flat of the blade, but not on an edge. Some can maneuver adequately when skating forward but not when skating backward. Others can balance well when skating slowly but not rapidly, or vice versa, or are competent when skating counterclockwise but flounder when attempting clockwise curves. Still others skate well while icebound but have trouble recovering their balance or their stride from a jump off the ice.

Lack of balance when skating backward is a common and often serious weakness. All players, not only defenders, should strive for excellent balance on all backward skating moves. This will give them greater versatility in game situations.

Balance is largely controlled by upper-body positioning and weight distribution over the skates. Proper development and use of the back muscles is critical. While the legs are the "engines" and are used for power and motion, the back muscles are used to hold the upper body still, and balanced, above the moving skates.

Goalies need to have superb balance. They often fall to the ice to make saves, then must return to their feet quickly. Good balance is necessary for these fast recoveries. Making a kick save without falling also requires excellent balance. Goalies who have not mastered balance often flop on all fours—not because they want to, but because they cannot stay on their feet. When this happens, they are slow to recover and are at the mercy of the opposition.

Falling and Getting Up

Everyone falls. The most important thing to remember is that you *must* protect your head from hitting the ice or the boards. Padding usually protects the rest of the body. When you feel yourself falling forward, quickly lift your head and chin as high as possible and look toward the ceiling. This is called "Heads-up Hockey" (USA Hockey). When you feel yourself falling over backward, tuck your chin into your chest to prevent your head from flipping back and hitting the ice.

Learning how to get up is initially challenging for beginning skaters. After you fall, get on all fours. Then put one knee on the ice and place the entire blade length of the other skate on the ice, directly under the center of your body. Keeping your back straight, use the flat of the blade to push down against the ice. After a few tries, you should be able to get up readily.

Balance on Two Skates

Balance on two skates is important when a player is gliding slowly—for example, when waiting for a pass or for a play to develop. It is also important when checking or being checked by an opponent. The following section teaches how to balance on the flats and edges of the skate blades.

Balance on the Flats of the Blades When Skating Forward

Figure 2.1 Proper balance

1. When gliding forward on the flats of both blades, hold your feet about shoulder-width apart and bend your knees. In this position you are stable and can easily prepare to thrust off (see chapter 4 for explanation).

2. Shoulders should always be held back. Concentrate on maintaining a vertical upper-body position by using your back muscles to keep your back straight. Look straight ahead and keep your head and eyes up. Slumping or looking down results in a loss of balance because it forces your body weight to pitch over the curved toes of the blades. Holding the upper body still is also critical for balance and control in skating.

3. Keep your body weight on the back halves of the blades which are from the middle to the heels.

4. Keep the skate blades in full contact with the ice. If you lift your heels off the ice, your weight pitches over the curved toes of the blades. Figure 2.1

illustrates proper balance; figure 2.2 illustrates what not to do. *Never* lean on your stick for balance or support. It is not a crutch or third leg!

a

b

Figure 2.2 *(a)* and *(b)* Result of slumping forward.

Balance on the Flats of the Blades When Skating Backward

The rules for forward balance on two skates apply also to backward balance, except that the body weight must be maintained farther forward on the blades—on the front halves of the blades—from middle to front, but *not* on the curved toes. Neither should you lean back. If your weight is on or behind the heels you'll fall over backward.

Balance on Two Skates on the Inside Edges

When gliding slowly forward or backward to wait for a play or pass, keep your feet somewhat wider apart than your shoulders, with both skates on the inside edges, and knees flexed (figure 2.3). This stance provides excellent stability. You are prepared to move laterally, straight ahead, or straight back. All you need to do to move is shift your weight onto the pushing foot and thrust off. Note: Even minimal inside edges provide more stability than the flats of the blades.

Figure 2.3 Gliding in wide stance on inside edges.

The more you dig in the inside edges and bend your knees, the more traction you will get into the ice and the more stable you will be. If you are about to be checked and do not have time to do anything else, widen your stance, dig in the inside edges, and bend your knees as much as possible. In this position you'll be much tougher to knock down.

Goalies almost always stand on the inside edges. Good balance on and knowing how to use the inside edges are extremely important skills for netminders.

Balance on One Skate

Skating is mainly a one-legged activity. Regardless of the maneuver being performed, only one skate is on the ice at a time. The body weight, therefore, is always totally committed to one skate. When pushing, the body weight must be totally balanced over the pushing skate. After pushing, the weight must transfer so that it is totally balanced over the gliding skate. In addition, you never know when you will be startled with a body check while on only one skate—for example, following a hard jolt—or when you will have to lunge, jump, evade, or leap over another player and land on one skate.

Balance on one skate must be mastered whether skating forward or backward, crossing over, starting, or turning. Learn to balance on the flat of the blade first and then on inside and outside edges. You will not be a proficient player until you can be perfectly comfortable on one skate—whether skating forward or backward, whether on the flat or on an edge.

Balance on One Skate on the Flat of the Blade

Figure 2.4 Proper balance on flat of the blade.

Balancing on the flat of the blade can be compared to balancing on a tightrope; all your weight must be directly over the gliding skate, with the full blade in contact with the ice. Place your weight solidly over the gliding skate so the skate cannot wiggle or move around (figure 2.4). Keep your hips facing straight ahead. If you lean to either side, or forward, or back, you may lose your footing—that is, fall off the tightrope.

Posture is critical to balance. Hold your shoulders back, and keep your back straight and unmoving. Look straight ahead with head and chin up. If your head and shoulders slump forward or if you look down, your weight will pitch over the curved toe of the blade and you will lose your balance.

Balance on One Skate on the Inside Edge of the Blade When Skating Forward

Balancing on an inside edge is more difficult than balancing on the flat, but it is essential. When gliding on an edge, imagine that you are gliding on a curved tightrope. Players glide on, shoot, check, and thrust from inside edges.

Lean your boot onto its side so the inside edge forms a 45-degree angle to the ice, and then stand on the edge in that position. Impossible? Maybe at first. But with enough practice, you will eventually be able to balance comfortably on a single edge. You will in fact find it not only possible, but a vital prerequisite to skating effectively.

To skate and balance on the inside edge of your left skate (LFI), lean the left boot, knee, and thigh strongly toward the center of your body so the inside edge cuts into the ice at a sharp angle. An effective angle at high speeds is 45 degrees. Using the right skate to push, thrust off and glide forward on the left inside edge. Lift your right foot off the ice after you thrust and hold it close to the skating foot as you glide on the inside edge (figure 2.5). Keep the skating (left) knee deeply bent with your body weight on the back half of the blade, and keep your hips facing the direction of travel. You will curve in a clockwise direction. Remember: The more you lean the skate, knee, and thigh, the tighter the curve or circle.

To do this on the right foot (RFI), mirror the procedure. You will curve in a counterclockwise direction.

Figure 2.5 Skating forward on left inside edge.

Note: This exercise should also be applied when practicing the forward stride.

Figure 2.6 Skating forward on left outside edge.

Balance on One Skate on the Outside Edge of the Blade When Skating Forward

Balancing on the outside edge is initially more difficult than balancing on either the flat or the inside edge. Regardless of its difficulty, it is an essential aspect of accelerating on a curve or circle.

To skate and balance on the outside edge of your left foot (LFO), lean the left skate, knee, and thigh strongly toward the outside (left) of your body so the outside edge cuts into the ice at a strong angle. An effective angle at high speeds is 45 degrees. Using the right skate as the pushing skate, thrust off and glide forward on the left outside edge. Lift your right foot off the ice after you thrust and hold it close to the skating foot as you glide on the outside edge (figure 2.6). Keep the skating knee deeply bent with your body weight on the back half of the blade. You will curve in a counterclockwise direction.

To do this on the right foot (RFO), mirror the procedure. You will curve in a clockwise direction.

Note: This exercise should also be applied when practicing forward crossovers.

Balance on One Skate on the Inside and Outside Edges When Skating Backward

Hockey players must be able to skate and balance on one edge as effectively during backward moves as when skating forward. To balance while skating backward on one skate on an inside or outside edge, the procedure is essentially the same as for forward skating, with two major differences:

1. Your weight must be on the front half of the blade (middle to front) rather than on the back half.

2. The direction of curve is opposite that produced by forward edges. See the section on gliding in chapter 1 (pages 8 and 9) for the directions of travel.

Note: All the previous exercises for inside and outside edges should be applied when practicing the backward stride and backward crossovers.

Coaching Tip

Shoulders should always be level to the ice. Dropping the inside shoulder into the circle is a common error. This tilts too much body weight into the circle, resulting in a loss of balance. It's safer to keep the inside shoulder slightly higher than the outside shoulder when skating on a sharp curve or circle.

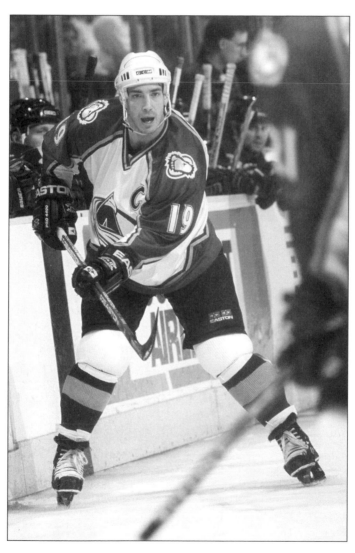

Joe Sakic demonstrates the wide-based stance used while waiting for a pass. He's on slight inside edges.

Combining Balance Exercises With Warm-up Exercises

Many balance exercises can also be used as warm-up exercises. When used in combination with warming up, they should be done as the first exercises of the day. Muscles require a chance to warm up and stretch gradually. If ice time is limited, these can be done off the ice, but they then do not help to develop better balance on the ice. Use balance exercises in combination with warming up and stretching on the ice whenever possible.

The exercises in this chapter help to improve balance, which should not be taken for granted. Balance is one of the first skills to deteriorate after even a brief layoff.

Unless otherwise specified, all exercises in this section can be executed while skating backward as well as forward. They are presented in a specific order that takes into account the need for gradual stretching.

Balance on the Flat of the Blade on One Skate

Quadriceps Stretch

Skate from the goal line to the near blue line with your hockey stick held horizontally at arm's length and at shoulder height in front of you. At the blue line raise your right knee as high as possible toward the stick. Glide on your left skate on the flat of the blade. Try to glide all the way to the far goal line before putting your right foot down. Repeat the exercise, lifting your left knee and gliding on your right skate. Raising the knee of your free leg gradually stretches the quadriceps (thigh muscles).

Many skaters are able to balance better on one foot than on the other. Give extra attention to the weaker foot to equalize right and left sides.

Balance on the Inside Edge on One Skate

Quadriceps Stretch

1. Skate forward on the RFI with hockey stick held horizontally at arm's length and at shoulder height in front of you. Raise your left knee up toward the stick. See how long you can glide on the RFI before putting your right foot down. You will curve in a counterclockwise direction (figure 2.7).

Figure 2.7 Balance on the inside edge (quadriceps stretch).

2. Reverse the exercise, skating forward on the LFI in a clockwise direction.

3. Repeat steps 1 and 2, this time skating backward on the RBI and then on the LBI. When skating on the RBI you will travel a clockwise curve. When skating on the LBI you will travel a counterclockwise curve.

4. Skate a complete circle on the RBI, and then on the LBI. Remember that the lean into the circle comes from the skating foot, knee, and thigh. If your upper body (chest and shoulders) leans into the circle, you will have too much weight pitching into the circle and you will lose your balance.

Balance on the Outside Edge on One Skate

Quadriceps Stretch

1. Skate forward on the LFO with hockey stick held horizontally at arm's length and at shoulder height in front of you. Raise your right knee up to the stick. See how long you can glide on the LFO before putting your right foot down. You will curve in a counterclockwise direction (figure 2.8)

2. Reverse the exercise, skating forward on the RFO in a clockwise direction.

3. Repeat the exercise, skating backward on the LBO and then on the RBO. When skating on the LBO you will travel a clockwise curve; you will travel counterclockwise when skating on the RBO.

Figure 2.8 Balance on the outside edge (quadriceps stretch).

4. Skate a complete circle on the LFO and then on the RFO. Remember that the lean into the circle comes from your skating foot, knee, and thigh. Your upper body (chest and shoulders) must not tilt into the circle. If it does, you will be off-balance.

5. Repeat, skating a complete circle backward on the LBO, then on the RBO.

Balance on the Flats of the Blades

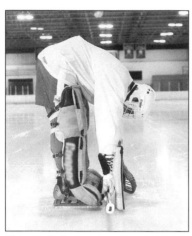

Figure 2.9 Hamstring stretch.

Hamstring Stretch

Glide forward on both skates, feet shoulder-width apart. Hold the hockey stick horizontally above your head. Then bend down and reach toward your toes with the stick, keeping your knees fairly straight and your weight on the back halves of the blades (figure 2.9). Do the same exercise gliding backward, with your weight now on the front halves of the blades. Always keep the entire blade lengths in contact with the ice. If your heel comes off the ice, you may fall forward over your toes. Hold the stretch for approximately 10 seconds. *Do not bounce*, as this may cause muscle pulls.

Twists

Figure 2.10 Stretch for neck, back, and waist muscles.

Stretch for the Neck, Back, and Waist

Glide on both skates, feet about shoulder-width apart. Hold the hockey stick behind your neck with a hand on each end of the stick, and rotate your waist and arms from side to side (figure 2.10). While twisting, reach your right elbow toward your left knee. Hold the stretch, then reach your left elbow toward your right knee. Look toward the knee your elbow is reaching for.

Groin Stretch

This exercise is generally done skating forward. It can be done skating backward, but that variation is quite difficult so it is recommended for more advanced skaters.

Groin stretches must be done gently at first and gradually intensified. Since groin muscles are prone to injury, they must be thoroughly warmed up and stretched before hard skating or a game. This exercise is also excellent for improving balance and knee bend.

Glide on the right skate, on the flat of the blade. Bend your right knee as much as possible so that your buttocks are sitting close to the ice while stretching the left leg behind you. Drag the inside of the left *boot* on the ice with the left foot in a turned-out position (figure 2.11). Keep your shoulders back, back straight, and eyes and head up to maintain a vertical upper-body position. Hold the hockey stick in the top hand with the stick blade on the ice in front of you. Your weight must be on the back half of the gliding skate.

Repeat the exercise, alternating legs. Gradually stretch the extended leg farther back as you feel the groin muscles stretch out. Do not bounce.

Note: Keep the inside edge of the extended skate off the ice.

Figure 2.11   Groin stretch.

Forward O Drill

In this exercise, you'll have both skates on the ice and move both legs out and in simultaneously to create the letter O. This will help loosen the groin and inside thigh muscles (adductors) and improve your balance on inside edges.

Start with your skates in a V position, heels together, toes apart, on the inside edges of both skates. Bend your knees, keeping your weight on the back halves of the blades (figure 2.12a). Move the toes of both skates as far apart as possible as you move forward. As your toes separate, straighten your knees (figure 2.12b). Then turn your toes inward and slowly draw them together (figure 2.12c). When your toes touch each other in an inverted-V position, you will have completed one full circle, or letter O (figure 2.12d). Put the heels of your skates together in the original V position and repeat the maneuver.

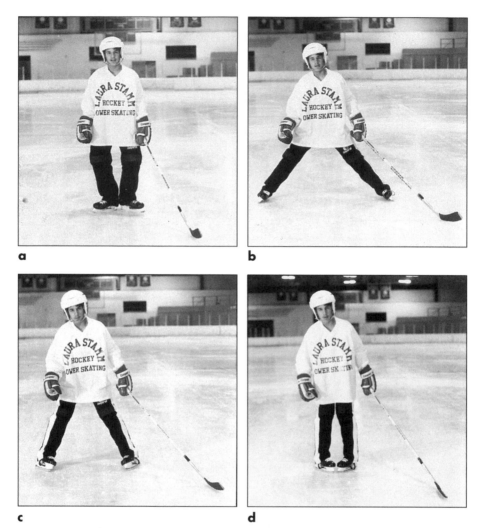

Figure 2.12 Forward O drill *(a-d)*. Backward O drill *(d-a)*.

Backward O Drill

This procedure is the reverse of the previous exercise. Start with your skates in an inverted-V position, toes touching, heels apart, on the inside edges. Bend your knees, keeping your weight on the front halves of the blades. Pull your heels as far apart as possible as you move backward. As your heels separate, straighten your knees. Then draw the heels together to form the letter V. After your heels touch, you will have completed one full circle, or letter O. Now bring your toes together in the original inverted-V position and repeat the maneuver (see figure 2.12 d-a).

Leg Lifts

Leg lifts must be done gently at first to gradually stretch the hamstrings, quadriceps, groin, and gluteal muscles.

1. Glide forward on the left skate, holding the hockey stick in front of you horizontally at shoulder height. See how long you can glide while keeping your right leg raised straight out in front of you and parallel to the ice (figure 2.13a). Do the same on your right skate, lifting your left leg. Beginners should glide on the flat of the blade. Advanced skaters can glide on the edges for a more difficult test of balance.

2. Glide forward on the left skate, on the flat of the blade. Hold the stick horizontally in front of you at shoulder height. Lift the right leg up and try to reach that foot to the stick (figure 2.13b). Repeat, balancing on the right skate and lifting your left leg.

3. Glide forward on the flat of the left skate. Still holding the hockey stick horizontally in front of you at shoulder height, lift the right leg up so that the right foot is close to or touching the stick in front of you (figure 2.13b). Bring the right foot down until your feet are together or touching (each other but not the ice). Now lift the right leg out to the

Figure 2.13 Leg lifts: *(a)* and *(b)* to the front; *(c)* to the side; and *(d)* to the back.

a

b

c

d

side (figure 2.13c). Bring the right foot down until your feet are close together or touching (each other but not the ice). Now lift the right leg straight behind you (figure 2.13d). Bring the right foot down until your feet are close together or touching (each other but not the ice). Repeat, lifting the left leg.

Keep the lifted leg as straight as possible for optimum stretching. When lifting to the front, you stretch the hamstrings. When lifting to the side, you stretch the groin muscles. When lifting to the back, you stretch the quadriceps and gluteal muscles. Lift as high as is comfortable, but be careful not to kick!

Repeat, now skating backward.

Note: Since this is also a balance exercise, do not let the foot that is off the ice touch the ice between lifts.

Plane Glide

Skate forward. Extend the hockey stick horizontally in front of you. Glide forward on the left skate with your right leg lifted behind you. Keep it straight and parallel to the ice. See how long you can hold this position without putting the right skate down on the ice. It is harder to balance with the free leg behind you than in front of you (look at figure 2.13d to see the proper position). Beginners should do this gliding on the flat of the blade; advanced players may glide on both the inside and outside edges. Figure 2.14 illustrates the exercise skating forward (a and b) and backward (c and d).

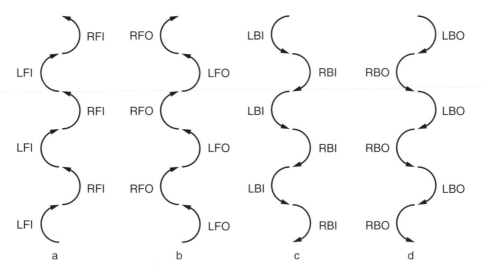

Figure 2.14 Plane glide, *alternating feet.* (a and b) forward (c and d) backward.

Toe Touch

Glide forward on the flat of your left skate, holding your hockey stick in one hand. Stretch your right leg horizontally behind you, lifting it so that it is straight and parallel to the ice. Keeping both legs as straight as possible, reach down and try to touch the toe of your skating foot. Repeat, gliding on the other foot. Be sure to keep the entire blade of the engaged skate in contact with the ice surface. If you allow the heel of the blade to lift off the ice, your weight will pitch over the curved toe and you may fall. Repeat the exercise, gliding backward.

This exercise demonstrates the importance of keeping the entire blade in contact with the ice. When skating backward your weight is primarily on the front half of the blade—but the entire blade length must be in contact with the ice or, as when performed skating forward, your weight will pitch over the curved toe.

Shoot the Duck

Squat over the right skate with your buttocks as close to the ice as possible. Your left leg should be off the ice, extended directly in front of you. Keep your back straight. If you lean too far forward from the waist, you won't be able to bend your knee to sit low enough. Experienced skaters should try to change feet while in this squatting position. Also, try to get up from this position without letting the free foot touch the ice. Try this exercise on each skate, backward as well as forward. This also is a good exercise for strengthening the quadriceps, one of the major muscle groups used in skating.

Jumps

This exercise is excellent for developing quadriceps strength and knee bend, as well as for improving balance on the flats of the blades. Practice this exercise both forward and backward.

Glide on two skates. At the first blue line, jump from and land on the flats of both skates. Continue jumping until you reach the far blue line.

Before each jump, bend your knees deeply so you are coiled to jump. Jump as high as possible. Cushion the landing by bending your knees deeply as you land. Keep your back straight as you land, and avoid the tendency to bend forward from the waist, as this will pitch your weight over the curved toes of the blades. Look straight ahead and keep your head up. Be sure to land so that the entire blade lengths of both skates are in contact with the ice.

Hops

This exercise is excellent for developing quadriceps strength and knee bend. It also helps develop balance and the recovery abilities often called for in game situations.

Glide on one skate. At the first blue line, begin hopping on one skate. Continue hopping on the same skate until you reach the far blue line. Keep the other foot off the ice throughout the exercise.

Before each hop, deeply bend the knee of the hopping leg so you are coiled to jump. Jump as high as possible. Cushion the landing by deeply bending the knee of the landing leg (figure 2.15, a-c). Keep your back straight as you land and avoid the tendency to bend forward from the waist, as this will pitch your weight over the curved toe of the blade. Look straight ahead and keep your head up. Be sure to land so that the entire blade length of the skate is in contact with the ice. Do the hops skating backward as well as forward, and be sure to hop equally on each foot.

a   b   c

Figure 2.15 Hops.

Forward Cross Lifts—Alternating Feet

Hold the hockey stick horizontally, chest high and fully extended in front of you. Glide forward on the right inside edge and lift the left leg off the ice and behind you (figure 2.16, a-b). Raise the left leg up to touch the hockey stick while changing to the outside edge of the skating foot (figure 2.16c) . Next, bring the left foot down onto the ice, crossed in front of the right foot. The left skate takes the ice on its inside edge (figure 2.16d). Then repeat the procedure while skating on the left foot, lifting the right leg off the ice and behind you and raising it to touch the stick. Change to the LFO as you lift the right leg up to touch the stick, and then bring the right skate down onto the ice, crossed in front of the left foot on its inside edge. Keep repeating the exercise. Note that the direction of travel changes as the edge changes.

Figure 2.16 *(a-d)* Forward cross lifts.

Backward Cross Lifts—Alternating Feet

Hold the hockey stick horizontally, chest high and fully extended in front of you. Glide backward on the right inside edge and lift the left leg off the ice and behind you (figure 2.17 a-b). Raise the left leg up to touch the hockey stick while changing to the outside edge of the skating foot (figure 2.17c). Next, bring the left foot down onto the ice, crossed in front of the right foot. The left skate takes the ice on its inside edge (figure 2.17d). Then repeat the procedure while skating on the left foot, lifting the right leg off the ice and behind you and raising it to touch the stick. Change to the LBO as you lift the right leg up to touch the stick, and then bring the right skate down onto the ice, crossed in front of the left foot on its inside edge. Keep repeating the exercise. Note that the line of travel changes as the edge changes.

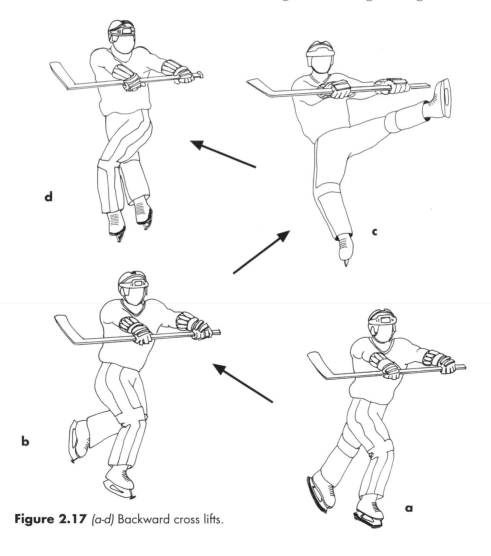

Figure 2.17 *(a-d)* Backward cross lifts.

chapter 3

Explosiveness Through Greater Force Application

Hockey is dominated by players who can skate *fast* and change direction at will. If you watch 20 of them, you will notice that each one has a unique style. While styles may differ, techniques are similar.

Every sport requires precise and controlled application of force. Explosive force, well timed and properly executed, results in movement, either of an object (such as a puck or ball), an opponent, or yourself. Certain principles must be followed to produce optimum force. Although the result in each sport may vary, the principles of force application are basically the same.

Speed is defined as distance covered in time. In hockey, it is measured by how far each stride carries the skater in a given time span. The time needed for a stride is approximated in fractions of a second. The distance covered depends on the correct, powerful, and explosive application of force. The time each stride takes depends on how rapidly the player changes feet (*leg turnover*).

Hockey is all about speed. To achieve it, one must apply the principles of force application—correctly, explosively, and with precise timing (power), and then combined with rapid leg movement.

Every stride consists of a push–glide sequence that involves a total transfer of body weight. Weight is first transferred from pushing edge to gliding edge and then from gliding edge (or flat) to pushing edge. Precise timing of the weight shifts is necessary for a smooth stride and efficient application of force.

Terms such as *wind-up, follow-through, coil, recoil, spring, release, drive, thrust,* and *explode* are commonly used throughout the sports world. These same terms effectively describe the basic components of hockey skating.

The motions of every skating stride can be broken down into four distinct segments. Every stride, like the swing of a baseball bat, requires a *wind-up* or coiling action, a *release* or application of force from the coiled position, and a *follow-through* or completion of momentum. Skating requires an additional move as well: a *return* or *recovery,* of the thrusting leg to a point centered under the body in preparation for the next stride. Try to separate every type of skating stride into these four segments: *wind-up, release, follow-through,* and *return.* When these principles are applied correctly, with power and quickness, you will skate faster.

The Wind-Up

In skating, the wind-up corresponds to the backswing of a baseball bat. It acts to "coil the spring." The more coiling action, the more force available upon release. This coiling action is achieved by digging in the edge of the thrusting skate at a strong angle to the ice (approximately 45 degrees), bending the knees (90 degrees), and pressing the body weight down over the gripping edge. This allows the edge to grip the ice strongly. There can be no traction without a strong thrusting edge or without the body weight pressing down over it. The skate will slip and slide rather than cut into the ice.

Figure 3.1   The wind-up.

The deeper the edge digs into the ice and the more the body weight presses downward over the edge, the more grip is available for the upcoming push (release). Figure 3.1 shows the wind-up of the forward stride, with inside edge, knee, and body weight pressing strongly downward toward the ice. The player pictured is prepared to push powerfully.

The Release

The release is the actual thrust. The pushing leg drives against the ice to move the skater. The release can be compared to the swing of a baseball bat—making contact with the ball causes the ball to move. The more efficiently and rapidly the legs thrust, the more power and speed the skater has. Many hockey players are unaware of just how hard their legs must push to get maximum speed.

During the release, the pushing leg, with the body weight concentrated over it, pushes powerfully, explosively, and directly against the cutting edge, which is wedged solidly into the ice (figure 3.2, a-b).

a   b

Figure 3.2   The release.

There is a general rule for thrusting that holds true for almost every type of skating maneuver: each push must be executed so that the thrusting leg pushes directly against the *entire length* of the blade, which is digging into the ice at an acute (approximately 45-degree) angle (figure 3.3, a-b). The thrusting blade may face different directions, depending on the specific maneuver, but the rule still applies. The leg must exert its force in a line perpendicular to that described by the blade's length—in other words, perpendicular to the grip. Figure 3.4, a-e shows the way the blade faces during various maneuvers and the resultant directions of leg drive.

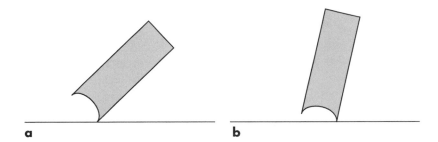

a   b

Figure 3.3   *(a)* a 45-degree angle of edge to ice sets up an effective thrust and allows the body weight to project low and forward; *(b)* a greater angle results in a weak push and causes upward body motion.

Remember that when thrusting you are actually pushing your entire weight against the cutting edge. The pushing leg does the work but the goal is to move yourself. To accomplish this your weight must be balanced over the thrusting leg for as long as possible. Only at the midpoint of the push should the body weight shift from the pushing skate to the gliding skate.

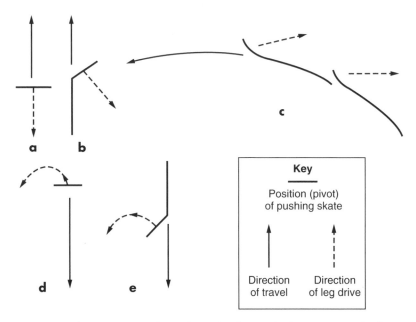

Figure 3.4 Pushing against the edge: *(a)* forward (front) start; *(b)* forward stride; *(c)* crossovers; *(d)* backward start; *(e)* backward stride.

The Follow-Through

Thrusting the legs without following through is like swinging the baseball bat and then halting the bat as it meets the ball (bunting). In skating, incomplete leg drive results in a significant loss of power, and therefore of distance covered on that stride.

Every push must finish with a follow-through. The thrusting leg is fully extended away from the body with the hip, thigh, knee, ankle, and toe locked. The gliding leg must maintain a deep knee bend as the thrusting leg extends. Only when fully extended, with the toe of the thrusting blade just barely off the ice, has the pushing leg followed through to its completion (figure 3.5, a-b). In backward skating, the thrusting skate, at full extension, actually stays on the ice.

Moving the legs overly fast is a common error that deprives the legs of the ability to reach full extension. So many players are encouraged to move their legs faster, faster. But each pushing leg *must* go through its full range of motion. It must reach full extension on the push, and recover totally on the return. Players whose strides are incomplete rarely reach their potential for speed and tend to tire more quickly. Their legs may go fast, but they don't. I call this "going nowhere fast."

a　　　　　　　　　　　　　　　　　**b**

Figure 3.5　The follow-through.

The range of motion is different for tall skaters than it is for short ones. In fact, it varies for each individual. First learn to thrust with complete leg drive for power, then practice this while trying to move your legs faster and faster. You may end up going faster with fewer strides.

> ### Coaching Tip
> Correct and powerful leg drive combined with rapid leg motion yields efficient speed.

The Return

Leg speed depends on how quickly a player changes feet. This, in turn, depends on a complete and rapid return (recovery)—how quickly the player is able to return the pushing leg and skate to the skate's position under the midpoint of the body.

After reaching full extension the thrusting leg and skate must return, retracing the outward path until the skate centers under the body. Only when the free leg and skate return to this position is the next leg prepared to push effectively. The body weight is now situated over the skate that is preparing to push.

The returning skate must stay close to the ice as it returns. In backward striding the skate actually stays on the ice during the return. On the forward stride, a straight-line path of return is most effective. A circular path takes longer, delaying the next stride. However, a circular path is necessary in backward striding because of the technique involved in the push and return portions of the stride.

A rapid return also requires that the knee of the gliding leg stays well bent during the return; this keeps the body weight low. Avoid popping or bouncing up between strides. Such pop-ups break forward momentum and cause a delay between strides.

The higher the returning skate lifts off the ice during the recovery phase, the longer it takes to change feet. Remember: Rapid leg turnover is critical to speed. Figure 3.6 a and b show a low and complete return during the forward stride. Figure 3.6c diagrams the straight line push/return of the forward stride.

a

b

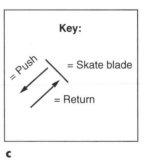

c

Figure 3.6 *(a)* and *(b)* complete return during the forward stride; *(c)* push/return of the forward stride.

chapter 4

Forward Stride for a More Aggressive Attack

How important is it for players to master the forward stride? Consider that the typical skater spends 85 percent of most hockey games skating straight ahead.

Great players seem to float over the ice, as though they were born with the gift of skating. While a few truly are natural skaters, most spend years perfecting their skating techniques.

Speed depends not only on rapid leg motion, but also on correct and powerful use of the blade edges, legs, and body weight. A serious misconception is that skating fast means moving the feet fast. Too many players are taught to move their feet fast regardless of *how* they move their feet or whether they are following the principles of force application. These players move as though on a treadmill, working hard but going nowhere.

Speed is a measure of distance traveled in a specific timeframe, say, miles per hour, feet per second. So whether skating forward or backward, crossing over, turning, or starting, you must cover distance on every stride. In other words, you always have to go somewhere.

All forward strides are technically alike. Neither the amount of force exerted on each thrust nor the techniques of leg drive, weight shift, and leg recovery vary. The basic difference is the length of the glide; how much time is spent on the glide skate before the next skate takes the ice to glide. To accelerate, glides must be short; but after having accelerated, it is important to maximize each glide. This will be discussed later in this chapter (see "The Glide of the Forward Stride," page 43).

The techniques of most hockey skating moves can be more easily applied after thoroughly understanding the techniques of the forward stride. Following is a detailed explanation of these techniques. They are explained for pushing with the right leg.

The Wind-Up

Power is generated when the wind-up starts from a point centered directly under the body (center of gravity). The center of gravity is an imaginary circle, about three inches in diameter, located in the midsection (belly button area) of the body. I refer to the center of gravity as the *battery pack* or *home base*. Each stride must begin and end under it.

1. The wind-up of each forward stride starts with the feet close together and centered under the body, with the feet pivoted outward and knees well bent (90 degrees). The feet and legs are in the V-diamond position. The heels are together but the knees are apart. The shape between the heels is a *V*; the shape between the ankles, knees, and thighs is a diamond. Figure 4.1a shows a wide *V*-diamond used when starting or skating slowly. Figure 4.1b shows a narrow *V*-diamond used when skating faster. Figure 4.1c diagrams the *V*-diamond position.

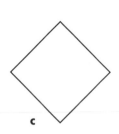

a

c

b

Figure 4.1 The V-diamond position: *(a)* wide V-diamond, *(b)* narrow V-diamond, *(c)* diagram of the V-diamond position.

Note: The *V*-diamond position is an integral part of other hockey maneuvers and is one of the most important positions to master. See "Turns and Transition," chapter 9.

2. With knees still well bent, press the inside edge of the thrusting (right) skate into the ice so the edge and lower leg form an approximate 45-degree angle with the ice.

3. With knees still well bent place your body weight to the inside of the thrusting skate and continue to lower your weight (figure 4.2a). At this instant your hips and chest should be positioned above the pushing skate.

The Release

When skating forward from a complete stop, or when skating very slowly, the angle of the pushing blade to the ice is approximately perpendicular to the line of travel and the push is approximately opposite to the direction of travel. The angle of the push decreases with speed; at top speeds the push is approximately 45 degrees from the direction of travel.

1. The release of the thrusting leg, directly out against the inside edge, is first to the back (behind you) and then to the side. The precise direction is determined by the way the blade edge faces on the ice (see figure 3.4, page 32).

2. Thrust directly against the grip, using the entire blade length to push. Start the push with the heel of the inside edge and finish with the toe of the inside edge (figure 4.2, b-c). This heel-to-toe push requires use of the entire length of the rockered blade: The body weight shifts from the back to the front of the inside edge during the push.

3. Although the leg performs the actual thrust, the purpose in pushing is to drive your total body weight against the blade edge that is gripping the ice.

4. The thigh muscles provide the main power of the thrust. If they don't feel the strain of each push, they are not being fully employed. Terms for pushing hard include *explode off the pushing leg, deliver a knockout punch, go full throttle,* and *gun the engine.* Hockey players get accustomed to pushing with a certain amount of force, believing it to be their maximum effort. However, most are capable of pushing much harder. Experimentation is essential for developing a more powerful and effective thrust.

5. Pushing to the back and side against a strongly gripping edge sets up the potential for a powerful push. Do not push straight back as in walking or running; this is not a skating motion. Pushing the leg straight back and finishing the push with the front tip of the blade are two of the most common errors in skating. They occur because a forward/backward leg motions is so natural. This motion along with using the front tip of the blade provides no traction and causes a slip against the ice rather than a thrust.

Skating = out/in, walking/running = back/forward.

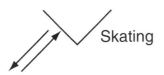 Skating

 Walking/running

6. During the thrust the entire blade length of the left skate takes the ice, receives the weight you are shifting from the pushing skate, and becomes the gliding skate. This transfer of weight onto the gliding skate takes place approximately midway through the push (figure 4.2b). If you shift your weight too early or if your weight is not shifted forward and outward completely over the gliding skate, momentum and power will be sacrificed.

Figure 4.2 Forward stride sequence: *(a)* wind-up, *(b)* release, *(c* and *d)* follow-through, *(e)* return, *(f)* wind-up, *(g)* release, *(h)* follow-through, *(i* and *j)* return.

Figure 4.2 *(continued)*

7. As it takes the ice, the new gliding skate aims slightly outward. Your body weight must shift outward as well, and must remain directly above the gliding skate for the duration of the glide. Toward the end of the glide there is a transition to what I call a "pre-pushing" phase. In this phase the gliding skate must be rolled onto its inside edge, and the body weight must shift inward and above it. Each glide therefore has two changes in weight—an outward weight shift followed by an inward weight shift. (See "The Glide of the Forward Stride," page 43.)

The Follow-Through

The push is not completed until the pushing leg reaches its full extension.

1. Continue thrusting against the inside edge until the pushing leg reaches its full extension. At the completion of the thrust, the hip and knee of the thrusting leg should snap into a locked position. This instant coincides with the *toe flick* (the final thrust from the front of the inside edge). This snapping

action of the toe against the ice at the finish of the push, combined with locking the pushing leg, gives the thrust its powerful finish (figure 4.2d). It is important to understand that the longer the pushing edge stays in contact with the ice, the more powerful the push will be.

2.   As the thrusting leg reaches its full extension and leaves the ice, it becomes the free leg. The act of lifting the skate from the ice is a natural continuation of the push.

3.   Keep the skate and knee of the free leg in a turned-out position, the toe within an inch of the ice (figure 4.2d). Raising the free skate much higher raises the center of gravity, breaks forward momentum, and delays leg recovery. "Toeing down," or pushing off with the tip of the toe instead of the inside edge of the toe (caused by loss of turnout of the knee and toe), results in the heel kicking up in a walking or running motion and prevents the toe flick from taking place.

4.   As the thrusting leg extends and becomes the free leg, the knee of the gliding leg should stay well bent (90 degrees). A deeply bent gliding knee will be out ahead of that same toe. If the gliding knee is straight or only moderately bent, the center of gravity will be too high. This hinders both stability and speed (figure 4.3 shows correct form; figure 4.4 shows incorrect). The amount of knee bend of the gliding leg also determines how far you can thrust the pushing leg against the ice and away from your body. A deep knee bend allows you to push longer and farther, maximizing speed and conserving energy.

Figure 4.3   Correct skating form with gliding knee bent strongly.

Figure 4.4   Incorrect skating form with gliding knee not bent sufficiently.

5.   At full extension there is a straight line of force from the shoulders through the thrusting hip, leg, ankle, and toe. At this instant the proper body position for the forward stride is as follows:

• Gliding knee ahead of gliding toe

• Chest over gliding knee

• Hips square (facing line of travel)

- Back straight
- Eyes straight ahead
- Head up and slightly ahead of the gliding knee
- Arms moving in line and in unison with the legs

At top speed the angle of the body (trunk) to the ice is approximately 45 degrees (figure 4.5).

Figure 4.5 Straight line of force and alignment of body at full extension.

The Return

The return of the free skate and leg coincides with the shift of the body weight over the inside edge of the gliding skate as it prepares to execute the next push.

1. To return (recover) the previous pushing (free) leg, pull it back until the free skate reaches a point directly under your center of gravity. This is done by reversing the leg's outward path. Keep the skate within an inch of the ice as it returns (figure 4.2e). The fastest and most effective way to move the legs in a sprinting push/recovery sequence is to follow a straight line path outward and inward.

In their haste to move their legs, players often fail to complete the return phase. They forget to pull the leg all the way back underneath home base. In skating, what goes out does not naturally come back in, but it *must* come back in. Think of *pulling* the skate and leg back in.

2. Keep the knee and toe of the free leg turned out during its recovery. In this turned-out position, the skates will be able to meet in the V-diamond position and be immediately prepared for the upcoming push–glide sequence.

3. Maintain a deep knee bend on the gliding leg during the return. Straightening the knee even slightly breaks forward momentum, slows the recovery process, and delays the next push.

4. As the free skate returns, it should momentarily meet the gliding skate with the skates and knees still in the V-diamond position and then immediately pass by it (about three-quarters of a blade length) to take the ice as the new gliding skate (figure 4.2f).

Note: On all skating strides the returning skate must move slightly ahead of the gliding skate before taking the ice as the new gliding skate. The returning skate moves forward, if skating forward, or backward, if skating backward, by approximately three-quarters of a blade length. This continuous progression of motion is an essential component of speed.

Execute the next push (left leg) as follows:

1. As the recovering skate draws under your body in the V-diamond position, the gliding skate is already pivoted outward and prepared to push. Dig the inside edge of the left skate into the ice at an approximately 45-degree angle, and bend both knees deeply.

2. Place your weight over the left inside edge and mirror with that leg the procedure of wind-up, release, follow-through, and return just described (figure 4.2, g-j). You have completed one cycle when you are again gliding on the original skate.

The One-Third, One-Third, One-Third Principle

This principle illustrates how important each element of the forward stride is to achieving speed.

For the purpose of generating power we may think of the skate blade as being divided into thirds: the back third or heel, middle third, and front third or toe. When skating at speed, power is equally generated: one-third from the heel, one-third from the middle, and one-third from the toe.

The First Third of the Push. The heel of the blade generates thrust only when the skate is directly under the center of gravity. Incomplete leg recovery disallows the first third of the push from the heel of the new pushing skate.

The Second Third of the Push. The middle of the blade generates thrust when the leg has already begun to push and is partially extended. Almost everyone manages to get this second third of the push.

The Third Third of the Push. The toe of the blade generates the final third of the thrust, but only when the pushing leg is fully extended with the accompanying toe flick.

Wide-based skaters who have incomplete leg recovery and who do not fully extend their legs or get a toe flick may lose up to two-thirds of their potential power on every push. These skaters work hard and accomplish little. They're the ones whose legs go a million miles an hour but who go nowhere fast.

The Glide of the Forward Stride

Is the initial glide of the forward stride on the flat or on the outside edge of the blade? This question is often debated. From the curved pattern of the glide it appears to glide initially on an outside edge. However, the outward curve could be a result of the outward direction of the gliding skate as it takes the ice and the subsequent transfer of body weight out over the blade.

If the glide actually does begin on the outside edge, the edge is minimal and of short duration. The edge changes almost immediately to the flat of the blade. The majority of the glide is on the flat. In preparation for pushing, the skate and body weight must rapidly shift inward and above the inside edge.

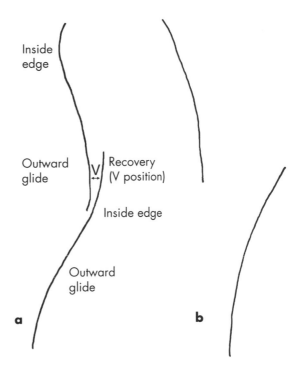

Figure 4.6 The glide of the forward stride: (a) correct, showing complete recovery with an outward/inward weight shift, (b) incorrect, showing incomplete leg recovery and a railroad track pattern.

Whether or not the initial glide is actually on the outside edge, try to skate as though it is, because an outside edge can *only* be achieved when the gliding skate takes the ice under the center of gravity. It requires that you return the free skate until it is completely centered under your body. This encourages efficient thrust, precise weight shift from pushing leg to gliding leg, and motion in the desired direction (figure 4.6a). Figure 4.6b shows strides that resemble railroad tracks. Railroad track strides are the result of incorrect and incomplete leg recovery. They create side to side, rather than forward, motion that wastes energy and inhibits forward speed.

The Arm Swing

Some skaters believe that swinging their arms vigorously makes them skate faster. But speed in skating comes primarily from the legs. The arms provide rhythm and momentum. They help increase speed when used correctly but they are not the prime source of speed. The arms are not a substitute for the legs—they should be used in addition them.

When game situations allow, players often carry their hockey sticks with just their top hand in order to swing their arms for additional speed.

Techniques of the Arm Swing

Move the arms forward and backward along diagonal lines in the same direction as and in rhythm with the legs. Arms must match legs in terms of force, direction of movement, and range of motion. As in running, the right arm drives forward as the right leg drives back.

- Each swing finishes with one arm extended diagonally forward and the other extended diagonally back, palms of both hands facing upward. An imaginary line is formed between the right hand and foot and between the left hand and foot (figure 4.7).

Figure 4.7   Correct arm swing: forward/ backward motion.

Figure 4.8   Incorrect arm swing: arms moving side to side.

- The elbows stay close to the ribs as they swing forward and backward. If they swing in a wide arc, the arms will move sideways and cross the midline of the body.
- The arms should *never* cross the midline of the body as this creates lateral instead of forward motion (figure 4.8).
- The upper body stays square to the line of travel. It does not twist from side to side. Shoulders move easily and stay level with the ice.
- Excessive churning of the arms is a waste of energy.
- The arms and legs work in unison; therefore, full arm extension encourages full leg extension. Short, choppy arm swings encourage short, choppy strides. Think of the wind-up of a softball pitch or bowling throw. A full backswing sets up forward motion on the throw. Similarly, in skating a full backswing helps drive the body weight forward.
- Many players are taught to always carry the hockey stick with both hands. In general this is sound advice, but there are also many instances when it is advantageous to carry the stick with

only the top hand. Consider the following scenarios in which carrying the stick with both hands is unnecessary and sometimes even disadvantageous.

Breakaways: In these situations you want to skate at top speed. By pushing the puck out ahead and swinging your arms, you increase speed. Skating while controlling the puck is almost always slower than skating with the stick in one hand and swinging the arms.

Breaking out without the puck: In these situations you try to get free, hoping to get into position to receive a pass.

Preparing to check an opponent into the boards: In these situations carrying the hockey stick in one hand and keeping it on the ice encourages a legal check, whereas carrying it in both hands with the stick off the ice may encourage an illegal check.

Skating fast: One example of this is when you are racing to get into position and at the same time want to establish a target to which a teammate can aim a pass.

Carrying the hockey stick in both hands while trying to skate fast almost ensures that you will lift the stick and swing the arms from side to side. Hockey coaches call this "pitching hay." I sometimes call it "cradling the baby."

If the stick is off the ice and the puck comes unexpectedly you may not be able to get the stick blade onto the ice quickly enough You might miss the puck. This happens at all levels of hockey and often in critical situations, and it helps the other team rather than your own.

Practice skating forward at speed, carrying the hockey stick in just your top hand. Keep the stick blade on the ice. Skate fast, pushing the puck out ahead of you. Extend your arms fully through their swing.

Note: The puck can be your best friend or your worst enemy. When you need to skate fast, it works to your advantage only if you keep it out in front of you. This allows you to bend your knees and angle your body well forward. If the puck is too close to your body, as can be the case when stickhandling, you have to straighten up and slow down because the puck blocks your forward motion. The rule for skating fast with the puck is that the puck goes first and you follow it.

Points to Remember

- Begin and end each push with skates and knees in the V-diamond position.
- Keep body weight low and angled forward for optimum forward motion.
- Keep gliding knee well bent throughout the stride for speed and momentum.

- Thrust the pushing leg to the back and side, directly against the entire blade length of the inside edge. Note: There is always some push to the back. You cannot move in one direction (forward) unless the push starts in the opposite direction (back).

- Begin each push with the pushing skate centered under your center of gravity. Finish each push with the thrusting leg fully extended away from your body.

- Prepare for the next push by returning that leg to a point directly under the center of gravity.

Note: The previous combined movements constitute full range of motion of the pushing leg.

- As the glide skate takes the ice, place the entire blade length of the glide skate on the ice. If you set down only the toe you will lose your balance.

- Once you learn to move the legs through their full range of motion, practice doing this at progressively faster tempos to achieve greater speed with fewer strides.

- Keep your hips square (facing straight ahead) and parallel with the ice.

- Look at the action and keep your head up. It's important to see what's going on all around you. Don't look down at the ice.

- Keep your head relatively still. Don't shake it from side to side.

- Keep shoulders back, chest up, and back straight. If you hunch over, your upper body is as strong as a wet noodle. You will be easily knocked down.

- Goalies must master all skating moves. The forward stride is especially important. The techniques for pushing across the goal crease are the same as those of the forward stride (figure 4.9, a-c).

Exercises for Improving the Forward Stride

The exercises for improving the forward stride are divided into exercises for each segment of the stride. Spend some time practicing them without and then with a puck. Once a puck is introduced, skating technique unfortunately deteriorates. Remember that in this book skating comes first; it is preferable to make puck-handling mistakes rather than skating mistakes. Skating correctly at speed while puckhandling is a skill that is honed only with years of practice.

a

b

c

Figure 4.9 Goalie using forward stride across goal crease (a) release (b) follow-through (c) recovery.

Wind-up Exercises

The purpose of these exercises is to practice executing the wind-up of the forward stride.

The Coil

The purpose of this exercise is to make you feel the amount of pressure needed to dig the edge into the ice at the angle needed to push effectively and the strain of maintaining that edge while the other foot is off the ice. Do the exercise first while standing in place, then while skating. Remember: Foot, skate, ankle, knee, and body weight must all work together to provide a strong cutting edge. The exercise is described for the right skate, but practice it equally on each skate.

Figure 4.10 The coil exercise: Balancing on the inside edge.

1. Place your skates and knees in the V-diamond position, heels together, toes apart.

2. Dig in the inside edge of the right skate and bend the right knee so that your skate, ankle, lower leg, and knee form a strong (45-degree) angle to the ice. The boot should lean halfway down to the ice.

3. Put all your weight on the right skate and lift your left foot.

4. Balance in place on the right inside edge. Apply strong inward pressure on the edge so that the edge angle does not change as you balance on it. The edge must not wobble from edge to flat and the blade must not move around (figure 4.10).

5. Now practice the exercise while gliding on the inside edge of each skate (figure 4.11).

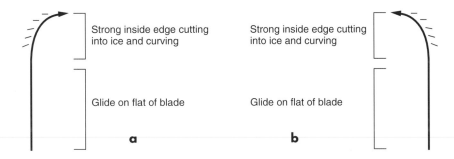

Figure 4.11 Flat-to-inside-edge exercise: *(a)* left skate and *(b)* right skate.

Flat to Inside Edge

This exercise is done skating at a slow to moderate pace; speed is not the goal. The idea is to develop the edging capability needed for an effective thrust. Do the exercise first with one skate, then with the other, with just one skate on the ice at any time.

1. Glide forward on the left skate, on the flat of the blade, right foot off the ice.

2. Keeping all your weight on the left skate, with your right foot still off the ice, quickly roll the left ankle inward and bend your left knee so that the inside edge cuts sharply (45-degree angle) into the ice.

3. The sudden cutting of the left inside edge into the ice will form a sharp semicircular curve in the ice; you will curve clockwise (figure 4.11a).

4. Now push off with your left leg and glide onto the flat of the right skate. Repeat the exercise on the right foot. The sudden cutting of the right inside edge will form a sharp counterclockwise curve (figure 4.11b).

5. Keep repeating, gliding on one skate, then the other, for the length of the ice. Figure 4.12 shows a player curving sharply on the inside edge of the right skate.

Figure 4.12 Player curving sharply on inside edge.

The action of going from the flat to a strong inside edge simulates that instant in the stride when the gliding skate rolls inward onto a strong inside edge in preparation for becoming the new thrusting skate.

Remember: If the blade does not roll in to a sufficient inside edge, the edge cannot cut into the ice. If this happens, the skate will have an insufficient grip and will skid as you attempt to push.

Release Exercises

The purpose of these exercises is to . . .

- help you practice executing an effective wind-up and release;
- improve your use of inside edges, knee bend, leg drive, and body weight; and
- help you practice pushing more powerfully and effectively.

Resistance Exercise

This exercise teaches you to dig into the ice more effectively and to push harder than you have had to before.

1. Partner up with another player. Face each other and stand along the sideboards, holding a hockey stick horizontally between you. Prepare to skate forward and push the other player across the ice.

2. The backward skater should resist the forward skater's movement by braking with a two-foot backward snowplow (described in chapter 8, pages 138 and 139).

3. To move the resisting skater, you, the player skating forward, must turn your skates and knees into an exaggerated V-diamond position. Dig in strongly with the inside edges and bend your knees. Place your weight over the pushing skate and concentrate it downward toward the ice.

4. Drive each push to full extension and return each skate and leg to the V-diamm position in order to prepare for the next thrust.

It is important that your partner give you enough resistance so that you have to work exceptionally hard to move, but not so much that you cannot move at all. Only with strong edging, knee bend, and leg drive should you be able to move the backward skater across the ice. The idea is that you, the forward skater, are challenged to use edges, legs, and body weight both correctly and forcefully in order to move your resisting partner. Keep your shoulders back, with your chest and head up, as you push the other player across the ice (figure 4.13).

Don't try to go fast. The object of the exercise is to feel the working of the edges, knees, legs, and body weight; to develop powerful leg drive and to become accustomed to feeling the cutting action of the blades before each thrust. When skating normally, you should use the same amount of edge, downward concentration of weight, and leg drive as you do when pushing a resisting skater.

Note: The previous exercise can also be used for practicing the windup and follow-through.

Figure 4.13 Resistance exercise.

One-Leg Push

Start from the sideboards and skate forward across the ice. Push each time with the right leg. To prepare for each push, dig the inside edge of the right skate into the ice at a 45-degree angle, bend the pushing knee deeply, and concentrate your body weight downward and above the edge as in the previous exercise. Thrust as hard as you can, to full extension, on every push. Return the skate and leg to the V-diamond position under the center of gravity before pushing again.

Coming back across the ice, use only the left leg to push. Many skaters are stronger and more coordinated on one side of the body than the other, so one leg often thrusts more powerfully. The idea is for both legs to eventually become equal in power and effectiveness. Repetition of these drills will help accomplish this. Remember, always emphasize the weak side.

Variation

Do the same drill, using only four pushes to reach the opposite boards. Recover the pushing leg rapidly but completely after each thrust to avoid excessive gliding. The goal is to build up speed on each of the four pushes so that after each push you are traveling faster than you were on the previous push.

One-Leg Drag/Touch

Do the previous exercise, but on each stride, drag the front of the inside edge (the toe) on the ice at the finish of the push. Keep the toe of the blade on the ice and drag the skate as it returns to center under your body. On the return the heel of the returning skate must touch (make contact with) the heel of the gliding skate in the V-diamond position. Keep the knee of the gliding leg well bent during the return. Maintain the turnout of the knee and toe of the returning leg.

Start from one sideboards. Skating across the ice, do the one-leg drag/touch pushes with the right leg. Coming back across, do them each time with the left leg.

Follow-Through Exercises

Use these exercises to practice executing an effective follow-through.

Snap/Stretch

On every forward skating stride, the muscles of the pushing leg—buttocks, hip, thigh, knee, ankle, and toe—must tighten at the very instant when the leg is locked and fully extended. This tightening indicates that the pushing leg has reached its complete extension, and that the toe has pushed against the ice to achieve the toe flick.

The purpose of this drill is to teach you the feeling of full leg extension. It is done standing in place.

1. Stand in the V-diamond position; heels together, toes apart.
2. Bend both knees deeply, keeping your back straight (figure 4.14a).
3. Quickly straighten both legs so that both knees lock. Hold your legs locked and feel the tightness in your leg muscles. There should be no crease behind your knees (figure 4.14b). This is how the pushing leg should feel when it is fully extended.
4. Repeat the exercise but this time keep the knee of one leg well bent and snap the other (pushing) leg to the back and side until it is locked. Keep the inside edge of the toe on the ice when the leg is snapped at full extension. When locked, the leg is in the position of the fully

 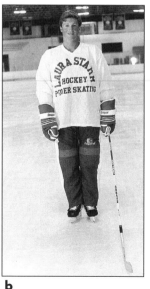 

a   b   c

Figure 4.14 Snap/stretch exercise. *(a)* coil in V-diamond position; *(b)* snap legs into locked position; *(c)* one leg bent, other leg locked.

extended leg during the forward stride (figure 4.14c). Hold the leg locked until you feel the tightness of the leg muscles and the amount of stretch between the bent (gliding) and extended (pushing) legs. Be sure to keep the knee and toe of the pushing leg in the turned-out position. Repeat with the other leg.

Bend/Extend

The purpose of this exercise is to practice keeping the knee of the gliding leg bent while the free leg is fully extended.

1. Start from the goal line and skate forward to the first blue line.

2. At the blue line, thrust the right leg against the inside edge, and glide on the left skate. Maintain a deep (90-degree) bend of the gliding knee

Figure 4.15 Bend/extend exercise.

(knee ahead of the toe). Thrust the right leg to full extension and hold it in that position with the right knee locked, knee and toe turned out, and the toe about one inch off the ice (figure 4.15).

3. Incline your body forward at an angle so that your chest lines up above the gliding (left) knee. Keep your back straight, chest and head up.

4. Hold this position as you glide on the left skate to the far blue line. When you reach the far blue line resume skating to the far end of the ice.

5. Hold the hockey stick with just the top hand and practice swinging your arms forward and back as you skate to the far end of the ice.

6. Repeat the exercise skating back down the ice, but now use the left leg as the thrusting leg and the right leg as the gliding leg.

Resistance

The resistance exercise described on page 50 can also be used as a follow-through exercise. Perform it in the same way.

Drag/Touch

This exercise has several functions in practicing the forward stride. It is a "feeling" exercise—it teaches you to

- feel the leg muscles lock when the pushing leg is fully extended,
- feel how to use the toe flick to finish each push properly,
- feel the correct "straight out/straight in" motions of the push/recovery sequence, and
- feel the difference between correct and incorrect leg motion.

This has been my favorite exercise for 30 years. I created it and I've used it to improve the forward stride of thousands of hockey players, novice to pro. This is one of my signature drills.

Other teachers recognize how uniquely suited this drill is to mastering the motions of the forward stride; they use it as well. I have never discovered another drill to be as perfectly suited to teach players the fundamentals of the forward stride. Many of my former pro students still tell me this was the best drill ever. This drill helped to fine-tune their forward stride more than any other.

I call the drill "drag/touch" when I want to abbreviate it. Its full name is "drag your toes, touch your heels." Learn it, then practice it properly and diligently. The most important thing to remember is that once you can execute the drill correctly, you must train yourself to skate the same way!

In this drill every push must begin and end in the V-diamond position.

After pushing off, fully extend the pushing (left) leg and drag the first two or three inches of the left inside edge (the "toe") on the ice for about two seconds (figure 4.16a). In order to drag the inside edge of the toe you must keep the left hip, leg, and toe turned outward. If they rotate inward, the toe will point straight down at the ice (toe down, heel up) and you will be forced

a   b

Figure 4.16 Drag/touch exercise: *(a)* drag; *(b)* touch.

to drag the "tiptoe" of the skate. The pushing leg will slip rather than grip because the skate is in a walking/running position.

After dragging the toe in the turned-out position, drag the heel of the returning (left) skate back under your body until it touches the heel of the gliding (right) skate. Your skates and knees should be in the V-diamond position, heels of the skates touching, toes apart (figure 4.16b). Keep the knee of the gliding leg well bent as the free leg returns.

Repeat, now pushing the right leg to full extension. When the right leg reaches full extension, drag the toe of that skate for two seconds before dragging that heel back to touch the heel of the gliding skate. Your skates and knees should once again be in the V-diamond position.

The purpose of dragging the toes and touching the heels is to enable you to *feel* the difference between correct and incorrect execution at every instant of the push/recovery sequence. It's much easier to feel the difference between right and wrong with your skates on the ice than when your skates are off the ice.

Repeat this drill slowly until you can feel each motion of the forward stride and can distinguish between correct and incorrect execution at every step along the way. Now, do the drill skating a bit faster.

Combine this exercise with two progressions:

1. Stride/Touch. This is the next step in the progression of developing a proper forward stride. This drill combines the forward stride push with the heel touch recovery.

Finish each push as if it were a normal forward stride push. Lift the fully extended skate so that the toe is within an inch of the ice. Return the skate under your body. During the return, keep the skate within an inch of the ice. On the completion of the return, *do* touch your heels together in the V-diamond position.

2. Stride. This is the next step in the progression. It is the actual forward stride. No longer will you drag your toes or touch your heels, but you will incorporate all the elements of the Drag/Touch drill to create an identically executed stride.

When completing the return of the free skate, the heels of your skates should be no farther than one inch apart, skates and knees in the V-diamond position.

Note: The only difference between the forward stride and the Drag/Touch drill is one inch of lift at the finish of each push and one inch of distance between the heels on each recovery.

Now skate fast, striving for perfect execution. Keep your skates close to the ice through each push/return sequence. Apply the techniques learned in the Drag/Touch drill, as they are the exact techniques of the forward stride. Swing your arms properly and completely.

Variation

Resistance drag/touch. Perform the resistance exercise on page 50 but drag your toes and touch your heels on each push/recovery sequence.

Forward C-Cuts

I created this exercise, and the term C-cuts, in 1971 and it was described in my first book, *Power Skating the Hockey Way.* C-cuts remain one of my signature drills to this day. The term is now commonly used by hockey and skating coaches everywhere to describe this push. I named the push a C-cut because in executing the push, the skate scribes a cut in the ice that is similar to the letter C (a semicircular arc). The C-cut push is used for backward as well as forward skating moves. When done properly it is a very powerful push and provides the player with many options.

In executing a forward C-cut, push the pushing leg first moves to the back; then it curves out to extend sideways, moves forward, and completes the C by curving back to its starting position beneath the midline of the body.

The C-cut exercise incorporates numerous important skating and training fundamentals:

- Using the inside edges to cut powerfully and forcefully into the ice when pushing
- Thrusting first to the back and then to the side rather than directly back
- Training the body to experience a fully extended, straightened free leg and a maximum-effort thrust, rather than a partially extended, weaker push
- Coordination—training the gliding and pushing legs to work independently of each other; while the glide is straight forward on a well-bent knee, the push is semicircular and the leg extends fully at the completion of the push.
- Using the heel to begin each push of the forward stride. Too many skaters do not properly use the heel to begin each push. The toe of the blade is not used in a C-cut push. You will only push with the back half of the blade.

Note: In all skating maneuvers, controlling the body weight over the rockered blade is as important as controlling the edges. As you learn to distribute your weight on specific points along the rock of the blade, you will develop greater agility and maneuverability.

- Determining the difference in effectiveness and coordination between the strong and weak leg so that you can practice equalizing them

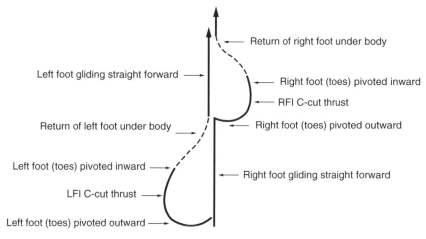

Figure 4.17 Pattern of the forward C-cut.

- Conditioning the quadriceps. The C-cut exercise employs the thigh muscles and forces them to work exceptionally hard
- Learning to execute the C-cut push of the backward stride. The push–glide sequence of backward C-cuts is exactly the reverse of forward C-cuts (see chapter 5, page 70)
- Preparing for more difficult maneuvers, such as tight turns, pivots, and bulling (see chapter 9), that incorporate forward C-cuts

The forward C-cut forms an upside down letter C. In other words, the push begins at the bottom of the C and ends at the top of the C.

The forward C-cut is skated with both skates on the ice at all times.

The exercise is described for the left leg as the initial pushing leg. It is diagrammed in figure 4.17.

1. Glide forward on the flats of both skates, feet directly under your body. Keep your back straight.
2. Prepare to push with the left leg while gliding straight ahead on the flat of the right skate.
3. Keep your weight on the back half of the thrusting (left) skate.
4. Bend your knees and dig the inside edge of the left skate into the ice so the skate and knee form a 45-degree angle to the ice. Concentrate your body weight over the edge.
5. Pivot the left foot outward with toe facing out to the side, so that your skates approximate a right angle. Heels will be together and toes will be apart (figure 4.18a). You are now prepared to execute a C-cut push.

6. Cut (push) the letter C into the ice with the left skate by pushing to the back, then outward until the pushing leg is fully extended out to the side (figures 4.18, b and c).

7. At the midpoint of the C-cut thrust, transfer your weight onto the right skate, which is gliding straight ahead on the flat of the blade.

8. Thrust powerfully and to full extension. Keep the thrusting skate on the ice after the thrust is completed. Note that the knee of the gliding leg remains well bent even when the thrusting leg is fully extended.

9. After the left leg reaches its full extension, re-pivot the left skate. The left toe should now face inward (pigeon-toed) toward the gliding skate. This step is necessary in order to return the skate to its starting position under your body (figure 4.18d).

10. Move the left leg forward and then inward to its starting position centered underneath your body (figure 4.18e).

Figure 4.18 Forward C-cut sequence: *(a)* pivot, *(b)* push, *(c)* full extension, *(d)* re-pivot, *(e)* return.

11. After the return your feet should be side by side and centered under your body.

12. After returning, the left skate becomes the new gliding skate. To push again, place your weight on the inside edge of the right skate and cut a reverse and upside down letter C with your right leg. Pivot the right skate, toe outward, and push first to the back, then out to the side to full extension. Then repivot the right skate (pigeon-toed) and bring it forward and then inward to its starting position centered under your body weight.

Note: Start the forward C-cut push at the bottom end of the C. Push first to the back, then out to the side, then forward, then finally around and inward to the starting point under the center of gravity.

Remember: The pushing leg must be locked and fully extended out to the side at the midpoint of the C, but it must be coiled and well centered under your body at the beginning and end points, which correspond respectively to the coil and return of each thrust, respectively. Keep the knee of the gliding leg well bent as you return the pushing leg.

Points to Remember

Following are some important points to remember when practicing the forward stride.

- Keep your hips facing straight ahead. If your hips turn sideways or wiggle you will skate from side to side like a snake rather than straight ahead. This will prevent you from achieving a full stride and will affect your forward motion.

- The push is a C-*cut*, not a silent C. The skate must *cut* into the ice; you should *hear* it. This indicates that your weight is over the pushing skate, with the inside edge gripping the ice strongly. A well executed C-cut is an extremely powerful push.

- The gliding skate must point straight ahead and glide on the flat of the blade as the thrusting foot pivots, cuts the C, re-pivots, and returns. If both skates turn the same way you will skate in a snake-like, "S" formation. Remember, the fastest way to travel between two points is a straight line!

- The initiation of every push is opposite from the direction of travel. The forward C-cut push is first to the back and then it continues out to the side.

- After reaching full extension, the push is completed. During the return, the skate no longer cuts into the ice. It glides back in to center under the body.

Figure 4.19 Forward C-cut, holding stick behind back.

• When skating forward from a stop or traveling very slowly, the direction of the push is almost perpendicular to and opposite the line of travel. The angle of the push decreases with speed: at top speeds the direction of the forward C-cut push is approximately 45 degrees from the line of travel.

Variation

Do the forward C-cut drill holding a hockey stick horizontally behind your back, in the crooks of your elbows (figure 4.19). Do not let the stick move around. This variation eliminates use of the arms and shoulders and forces the legs to do all the work.

Return Exercises

Use these exercises to practice the recovery phase of the forward stride.

Snap/Click

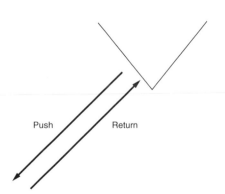

Figure 4.20 Push-return.

This exercise is done standing in place.

1. With the knee of your standing leg deeply bent, snap the pushing leg out to the back and side until it is locked and fully extended.

2. Return the pushing leg back under your body, until that heel clicks against the heel of the standing skate. As your heels click, the skates and knees should take the V-diamond position. It is important to maintain the turnout of the knee and toe through the return. Remember to return the leg so that it exactly reverses its outward path (figure 4.20).

3. Keep the knee of the standing leg well bent as the pushing leg returns and as your heels click together.

4. Repeat, using the other leg as the pushing leg.

5. Keep repeating the exercise to develop the correct return motion.

Note: Although the heels do not actually touch when striding, they should be no more than one inch apart.

Push/Click

Skate forward. On each stride concentrate on returning the pushing skate so that your heels click together, skates and knees in the V-diamond position. Be sure to drive the pushing leg directly against the inside edge and return it along a straight line that retraces its outward path (see figure 4.20).

The act of making the heels touch helps you develop the feeling of where your center of gravity is and when your skates are directly beneath it.

Stride Tempos: The Rapid Stride Versus the Long Stride

All strides should be *full* strides. The difference between a rapid stride and a long stride is leg speed; in other words, the amount of time spent gliding. Rapid strides are comparable to those in sprint running, when a sudden burst of speed over a relatively short distance is required.

The rapidity of strides is determined by how quickly the legs move as they push and recover and how quickly the legs change. This is referred to in hockey as *leg turnover.* The faster the legs change, the shorter the time spent gliding. Knee bend, edges, leg extension, and effort expended in pushing are the same. The thrusting leg must drive to full extension and return fully under the body even when leg motion is very rapid.

Hockey often requires very rapid strides, as when starting explosively, accelerating from slow to fast, or bursting out on a breakaway. There are, however, times when slower leg speed is called for: for example, when you have reached top speed and want to maintain it, or when you do not need to skate at top speed. In these situations the legs move somewhat slower, but the strides are technically the same.

Exercises for Stride Tempos

Since all strides are really long, or full, strides, we will refer to "long glides" rather than long strides. The main purpose of these exercises is to produce correct technique at varying stride tempos and to develop balance and control at all stride tempos.

Long Glides

This exercise is done as you skate around the entire rink. Pick up speed on the corners by using crossovers. As you approach the blue line, use rapid strides. At the first blue line thrust just once with the right leg and then glide on your left skate until you reach the red line. Keep the free leg fully extended until you reach the red line. At the red line, repeat, switching feet and legs. Thrust with the left leg and glide on your right skate, keeping the free leg fully extended until you reach the next blue line. The idea is to maintain speed and balance for the entire length of the glide. If you use the edges properly and thrust hard you should be able to maintain speed on the glide.

When you reach the second blue line use rapid strides to skate to the far end of the ice. Skate crossovers around the corners to build up speed again. When you are back at the first blue line on the other side of the ice, repeat the long glides. Move your arms diagonally forward and back in line and in rhythm with your legs. Keep the hockey stick on the ice, holding it with just your top hand. Reverse your direction around the rink and repeat the exercise. Always skate exercises involving crossovers in both directions.

Note: Small skaters should use two strides from blue line to red line, and two strides from red line to blue line.

Varying Stride Tempos

Start from the goal line and skate the length of the ice. Vary stride tempos as follows:

1. Between the goal line and the near blue line take 8 to 10 rapid strides.
2. From blue line to blue line take 4 strides.
3. Between far blue line and far goal line take only 2 strides.

Maintain speed even when doing the very long glides, and be sure you always push to full extension. Swing your arms diagonally forward and backward in line with and in rhythm with your legs. Keep the hockey stick on the ice, holding it with your top hand only.

The number of strides needed may vary. For example, younger players may need 12, 6, and 3 strides respectively, from goal line to blue line, blue line to blue line, and blue line to goal line. Advanced players may need fewer.

Stride and Control

This excellent exercise helps improve balance and control on glides and is similar to the exercise for long glides. Skate around the rink in a counterclockwise direction. Immediately after coming out of the corner and reaching the face-off circle push once (using the right leg to thrust and the left skate to glide) and glide all the way to the center red line. At the red line thrust once with the left leg and glide on the right skate until you reach the face-off circle at the far end of the ice. Skate hard and fast around the corner (crossovers) to build up speed, then repeat. Keep the free leg fully extended during the glides. Use powerful, rapid crossovers to build up speed on the corners. Try to maintain speed on the two long glides. Repeat the exercise, now skating in a clockwise direction.

Note: Because this exercise uses only two strides for the length of the ice (from face-off circle, to face-off circle it demands extremely powerful pushes and acceleration around the corners. Balance and upper body control are essential. Younger skaters may need to take four or six strides for each length of the ice. Again, the numbers are an approximation and depend on age and ability.

Rapid Leg Tempos

After learning to thrust properly and powerfully you may find that your legs push effectively but do not move quickly enough. The challenge for every player is to develop powerful and rapid leg tempos while maintaining correct technique.

Coaching Tip

In addition to quickness training (see chapter 11), skating to music is an effective way to develop varying leg tempos. Use music with increasingly fast rhythms. Try to move your legs in time to the music, but remember to get maximum power and full range of motion on each stride.

As your leg speeds increase, experiment using rhythms that put you temporarily out of control. This is called *over-speed skating* and is an essential part of hockey training. But remember, correct technique plus rapid leg speed is the goal. One without the other is inadequate.

Varying Leg Speeds

To improve versatility, practice skating powerfully to many different tempos of music. This will help you skate rhythmically. Swing your arms in a diagonal forward-backward motion, always in line and in rhythm with your legs.

Leg rhythm is slightly different for each person. Rhythm varies according to one's body type and leg length. Small and tall players have completely different styles and leg rhythms. If tall players move their legs too fast for their leg length, they reduce their ability to achieve full range of motion. Concentrate on developing powerful and rapid leg drive while still moving the legs through their full range of motion. Move your legs as rapidly as possible. But remember that leg rhythm is unique to each individual and must accommodate your body type and leg length.

Apply the previous exercises to all skating maneuvers.

Restricting the Arms

Restricting the use of the arms during stride exercises helps emphasize and develop correct use of the legs, especially when skating with two hands on the stick and controlling the puck. Too many players lose their stride when skating with the puck because they can't use their legs independently of their arms. The following exercises restrict arm movement and train the legs to work independently of the arms.

Exercise 1

Skate forward, holding the hockey stick horizontally behind your back in the crooks of your elbows. Or, use no stick at all and clasp your hands on your stomach or behind your back. You may also hold the stick horizontally with your arms extended straight out in front of you and chest high. Keep your upper body still and your chest facing straight ahead while skating in these positions.

Exercise 2

Figure 4.21 Restricting the arms by holding hockey stick with both hands.

Practice skating at top speed, holding the hockey stick with both hands and keeping the stick on the ice. Keep the stick out in front of you (figure 4.21). Practice without and then with the puck. Push powerfully and rapidly and try to achieve speed from your legs alone.

Once you can use your legs properly and powerfully without the aid of your arms, skate while holding the hockey stick in just your top hand. Keep the puck well in front of you but still on the ice. Swing your arms in a forward-backward motion, in line and rhythm with your legs (see figure 4.1b, page 36).

chapter 5

Backward Stride for Mobility on Defense

The ability to skate straight backward FAST is essential for all players, not just for defenders. All players are placed in defensive situations from time to time. If their backward speed is inadequate, the opposing team has a distinct advantage.

Some players like to use backward crossovers when skating backward. They feel they can go faster this way than when skating straight backward. However, backward crossovers can be dangerous when used improperly in game situations. Remember, defenders should never make the first move! Crossing over before the forward has committed to a direction translates to having made the first move.

Here are some examples of what can happen when a defender crosses over at the wrong time:

1. The forward with the puck races up the ice. The defender backs up, crossing over one way, then the other. Each backward crossover must be followed by a neutralizing step outward in the same direction in order to uncross the feet before the defender can take another step. The knowledge-able forward looks for this and immediately recognizes it as a great opportunity, quickly cuts the other way, and gets beyond the defender's reach.

2. The forward with the puck races up the ice. The defender backs up, planning to stay in front of the forward and prevent that forward from breaking free. The defender crosses over and puts his or her weight on the foot that crossed over. I call this the "pretzel syndrome" because the defender's feet are twisted like a pretzel. If the defender tries to cross the other foot over and go back in the original direction, it's a guaranteed fall. I've seen these blunders in critical games—twice even in Stanley Cup *final* games. Both times these mistakes caused opportunities for the forward; both times the forward scored the winning goal. Big mistake.

Coaching Tip
Defenders: Never make the first move.

Backward crossovers are an excellent way to accelerate from a stop, or to change gears from slow to fast. Once speed has been built up, players should use the straight backward stride to skate backward. By skating straight backward, defenders can more readily stay directly in front of oncoming forwards while keeping their feet in a neutral position. They have a better chance of staying with, tracking, and moving with opposing forwards to follow their direction and prevent their escape.

As in the forward stride, rapid leg turnover alone does not ensure speed. Correct technique and power, combined with rapid leg speed, is the critical combination.

The push of the backward stride is the C-cut push, done in reverse of the forward C-cut push described in chapter 4. In executing the backward C-cut the pushing leg first moves to the front (opposite the direction of travel), then out to the side to fully extend. It then moves back around and inward to its endpoint beneath the midline of the body. In other words, the push now starts from the top of the C and works down to the bottom of the C.

The four-part procedure of wind-up, release, follow-through, and return is as important to power and speed in the backward stride as it is in the forward stride. The proper use of edges, knee bend, leg drive, body weight, weight shift, arm swing, and glide so necessary for speed when skating forward is also necessary for speed when skating backward.

The Wind-Up

Each push begins with a coiling action. To initiate the push of the backward stride, the thrusting skate must be centered under the body (center of gravity) and must dig into the ice with a strong (45-degree) inside edge. Knees must be well bent and shoulders held back. The upper body should be held in an almost vertical position with body weight on the front halves of the blades.

1. Glide backward on the flats of both skates, feet directly under your body.
2. Prepare to push with the left leg. Place your weight above the pushing (left) skate and bend your knees deeply—the knee of the pushing skate should be out ahead of that toe.
3. Pivot the pushing (left) skate outward (heel facing out to the side) until your feet approximate a right angle or upside-down and reversed letter L (toes together, heels apart). Pivoting the pushing skate is critical to the C-cut thrust (figure 5.1).

4. Dig the inside edge of the pushing (left) skate into the ice by rolling in the ankle and bending the knee so that the skate and lower leg form a 45-degree angle to the ice. Your weight must be totally concentrated over the pushing skate. You are now prepared to execute the C-cut push.

Figure 5.1 Pivot of the backward C-cut.

The Release

1. Using the inside edge of the left skate, push (cut) the letter C into the ice. Use the front half of the blade to push. Start the push from the middle of the inside edge; finish with the toe of the inside edge. The push is an upside-down C; it starts from the top of the C and cuts first to the front, then out to the side. Drive the pushing leg powerfully against the edge, using a forceful snapping action of the leg (figure 5.2a).

2. At approximately the midpoint of the C-cut thrust, transfer your weight from the pushing skate onto the gliding (right) skate. Because you are skating backward, your body weight should be situated over the front half of the gliding skate. However, the *entire* blade length must be in contact with the ice.

3. Thrust the pushing leg to full extension (figure 5.2b). Push forcefully and explosively. Remember that as you push the inside edge must *cut* into the ice.

The Follow-Through

As in the forward stride, the push is only completed when the pushing leg reaches full extension.

1. The final thrust comes from the front of the inside edge (toe). The locking of the pushing leg coincides with the toe flick of the inside edge. This combination constitutes an effective follow-through (figure 5.2b). Trial and error is necessary for you to feel *your* point of full extension.

2. Keep the entire blade length of the thrusting (left) skate *on* the ice after the thrust is completed. If the heel lifts off the ice, the front tip of the blade may catch in the ice, causing a loss of balance and making the recovery phase difficult.

3. Keep the knee of the gliding leg well bent even when the thrusting leg is fully extended.

4. Keep the gliding skate pointing straight backward during the push and recovery phases.

5. Glide on the flat of the blade, keeping the entire blade length in contact with the ice. If the heel lifts off the ice, you will fall forward over the curved toe of the blade.

The Return

The return of the backward stride is often neglected (as it is when skating forward). It is an essential part of the stride because only *complete* leg recovery can set up a powerful next push.

1. After the thrusting leg reaches full extension, the leg must return rapidly to a position under the center of gravity in preparation for the next push. To return the skate and leg, re-pivot the left heel to face inward (figure 5.2c). This step is necessary in order to return the skate to its starting position under your body.

2. Draw (pull) the returning (left) skate under your center of gravity. A complete return of the pushing skate completes the C (figure 5.2d). Keep the entire blade length on the ice as the skate returns.

3. After the return your skates should be side by side and under your body. Do not allow the returning skate to move past or behind the gliding skate. This will pull your hips to the side, forcing you to move in a snakelike pattern.

4. After the return the left skate becomes the new gliding skate while the right skate is prepared to thrust (C-cut). The C must now be formed in reverse. Put your weight above the right skate, bend your knees, and pivot the right heel outward (figure 5.2e). Mirror the procedure of windup, release, follow-through, and return described previously for the left C-cut thrust to execute the right C-cut thrust to full extension (figure 5.2f).

Points to Remember

Following are some important points to remember when practicing the backward stride.

• The gliding leg travels a straight line backward while the pushing leg pushes and returns in a semicircular (C-shaped) motion.

Figure 5.2 Backward stride sequence: *(a)* release; (b) follow-through; *(c)* re-pivot; *(d)* return; *(e)* wind-up; *(f)* follow-through.

Coaching Tip

The fastest way to travel between two points is a straight line. Since the gliding skate determines direction, you will go where it travels. If both skates turn during the pivot and C-cut push, you will travel a snake-like S pattern. The push–glide sequence of the backward stride is diagrammed in figure 5.3.

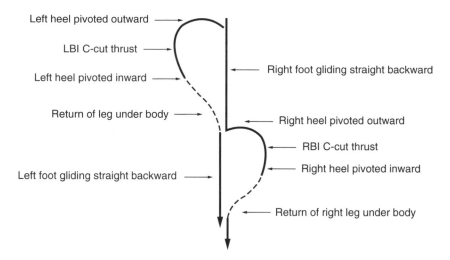

Left heel pivoted outward

LBI C-cut thrust

Left heel pivoted inward

Return of leg under body

Left foot gliding straight backward

Right foot gliding straight backward

Right heel pivoted outward

RBI C-cut thrust

Right heel pivoted inward

Return of right leg under body

Figure 5.3   Pattern of the backward C-cut.

- The directional skate must always be situated directly under the body weight in order to glide straight backward.

- The new gliding skate takes the ice slightly ahead of (behind you, when skating backward) where the previous skate had been gliding before it started to push.

Note: On all skating strides the new directional skate must move slightly ahead of the previous directional skate as it takes the ice to glide—forward if skating forward, or backward if skating backward—by approximately three-quarters of a blade length.

- Push the C-cut first to the front (forward) then out to the side. When skating backward from a complete stop or when traveling very slowly, the angle of the pushing blade to the ice is approximately perpendicular to the line of travel and the push is almost from the direction of travel. The angle of the push decreases with speed; at top speeds the direction of the backward C-cut push is 45 degrees from the line of travel. The precise direction is determined by the way the blade is facing on the ice.

- At the full extension of each push, the thrusting leg should be as far away from your body as it will reach, with that knee locked and the toe of the inside edge pushing against the ice. The toe flick provides the final thrust, just as it does in forward striding. Keep the knee of the gliding leg bent strongly to allow for a full thrust.

- The one-third, one-third, one-third principle does not apply when skating backward because the push is mainly from only the front half of the blade. If you miss the first half of the push (caused by incomplete leg recovery), you lose 50 percent of the push. If you lose the toe flick (caused by incomplete leg extension), you lose 50 percent. Correct and complete execution is imperative.

• Cut the C into the ice only to the point at which the pushing leg is fully extended. The return phase of the C is a glide, not a push. If you attempt to cut the ice during the second half of the C (the recovery phase) your hips will turn sideways and you will skate snake-like.

• Keep the entire blade lengths of both pushing and gliding skates in full contact with the ice. Lifting one or both heels off the ice causes the body to pitch forward over the curved toes.

• The knee of the thrusting leg snaps into the fully extended position at a point corresponding to the middle of the C. It must, however, be well bent and coiled under your body at the beginning and endpoints of the C, which correspond to the coil and return points, respectively, of the thrust.

• Keep shoulders back, back straight (almost vertical), eyes ahead, and head up. If you have to lean on your stick to prevent falling, you have either lifted your heels, leaned too far forward, dropped your head, or all of the above.

• Keep hips square (facing straight ahead) throughout the push–glide sequences. As in all skating, you travel where your hips face—so if you turn them sideways as you cut each C, you will waddle from side to side.

• Hold the hockey stick with just your top hand and keep the stick on the ice in front of you. Move your arms in a diagonal forward-backward direction, in line and in rhythm with your legs (as in the forward stride). As the left leg pushes to the front and side, the left arm drives back; as the right leg pushes to the front and side, the right arm drives back.

The Glide of the Backward Stride

The glide of the backward stride is the exact reverse of the glide of the forward stride. Likewise, you don't actually travel a straight line, but a slightly curved line as in the forward stride (see chapter 4). Figure 5.4a diagrams the actual glide-and-push pattern of the backward stride. Figure 5.4b diagrams an incorrect pattern, caused by turning both skates the same way during the push.

For learning purposes, practice traveling a straight line backward on the flat of the blade (along the desired line of travel) while the pushing leg executes the C-cut. Develop the coordination required so that the pushing and gliding legs can work independently rather than both moving the same way.

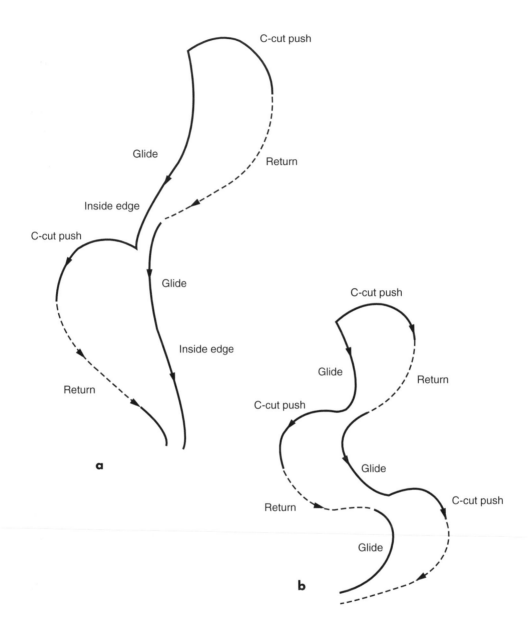

Figure 5.4 Glide of the backward stride: (*a*) correct; traveling straight back; (*b*) incorrect; traveling like a snake.

Stride Tempos

As in forward skating, all stride lengths and stride tempos must be equal. A stride in which one leg pushes fully and the other pushes only partially is insufficient. The same is true of a stride in which one leg moves rapidly and the other moves slowly.

Try to develop varying rhythms when striding backward (similar to forward striding) but remember that all strides should be full strides. Stride tempo depends on how quickly the free leg and skate return to beneath the center of gravity so that you can change feet. Practice correctly and slowly, then correctly faster, fastest, and even at speeds that put you out of control (over-speed training), first without a puck, then while controlling a puck.

Note: Tempo should not diminish the length of the push. As with the forward stride, experiment with varying musical tempos.

Exercises for Improving the Backward Stride

The following exercises, practiced repeatedly, help develop the skill, coordination, and power to become proficient at skating straight backward.

O Drill

This drill provides an elementary means for the learning skater to execute backward pushes. See chapter 2 (page 22) for directions for performing this exercise skating forward. Reverse the procedure described.

Backward C-Cut

Perform a series of C-cuts as you skate straight backward. Alternate pushing and gliding legs. Concentrate on executing the four parts of the C-cut—pivot, push, re-pivot, return. Dig in with a deep inside edge, use powerful leg drive, push to full extension, and always return the pushing skate to the center of gravity (under your body weight) before thrusting with the other leg. A good way to practice this exercise is to touch your skates together on the completion of each return. Be sure to keep the gliding skate pointing straight back throughout and maintain a deep knee bend at all times (see "Forward C-Cuts," chapter 4, page 56).

Resistance

Face another player and hold a stick between you. Holding on to one end of the stick with one hand, use backward C-cut thrusts to pull the resisting skater across the ice (figure 5.5, a-b). Be sure to aim the gliding skate straight backward while executing each C-cut push and return the pushing skate under the body. The forward skater should do a two-foot snowplow stop (see chapter 8, page 133) to resist movement. This forces the backward skater to exaggerate the use of knee bend, inside edges, leg drive, and full recovery.

a   b

Figure 5.5 Resistance exercise: (a) pivot and push; (b) full extension.

Hockey Stick Drill

This exercise trains the gliding skate to travel in a straight line backward while the thrusting skate pivots, executes the C-cut push, repivots, and returns.

1. Place a hockey stick on the ice.
2. Stand to the left of the stick and next to it.
3. Place the gliding (right) skate close to and parallel with the stick. Prepare to glide straight back on the flat of the right skate in a direction parallel to the stick.
4. Pivot the heel of your pushing (left) skate outward and bend your left knee deeply (figure 5.6a).
5. Execute one backward C-cut thrust with your left leg. Push to full extension while gliding straight backward on your right skate. Glide backward, keeping the right skate parallel with and next to the stick (figure 5.6b).

6. Continue to glide straight backward while returning the extended (left) skate under your body so that your heels actually touch (figure 5.6c).

7. Stop.

8. Repeat the exercise, now standing on the right side of the stick. The left skate will glide and the right skate will push. Cut one backward C-cut push with your right leg and glide straight backward on the left skate. After the right leg reaches full extension, re-pivot that skate and return it under your body until your heels touch each other.

9. Stop.

Keep repeating this procedure, alternating left and right C-cut pushes. Push each time from a complete standstill. Remember to keep your head up, back straight, and hips square to the line of travel.

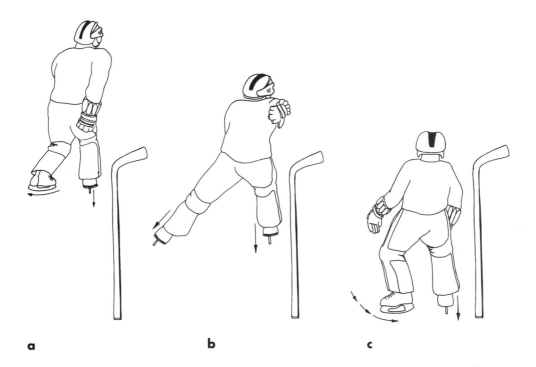

a   b   c

Figure 5.6 Hockey stick exercise *(a)* pivot and push; *(b)* full extension; *(c)* re-pivot and return.

One-Leg C-Cut

Do backward C-cut thrusts across the ice, pushing each time with your right leg. Coming back across the ice, do backward C-cut thrusts, pushing each time with your left leg; fully extend each push. Now try using only four pushes to take you completely across the ice (six for smaller skaters). Each thrust should make you go faster than the previous thrust. Be sure that the gliding skate always travels straight backward—don't zigzag.

The Return

To practice the return phase of the backward stride, repeat the previous four drills, but on every return make the heel of the returning skate actually touch (make contact with) the heel of the gliding skate.

Forward Versus Defender

Practice with another player by competing as a defender against a forward. The defender stands at the blue line and prepares to skate backward. The forward stands at the goal line directly opposite the defender and prepares to skate forward. Start simultaneously at a whistle signal. The object is for the defender to skate straight backward (no crossovers) and not to allow the forward to catch and pass him or her. Alternate with your partner so that both of you practice as forward and defender.

chapter 6

Crossovers for Acceleration on Curves

Crossovers are moves used to accelerate on curves, circles, and corners. They make it possible for players to weave in and out of traffic, zigzag down the ice, change direction, and move laterally (from side to side). Watch the agility of NHL stars such as Paul Kariya and Joe Sakic and you will see flawless and powerful crossovers. Powerful, fast crossovers are essential for every hockey player.

Practice forward and backward crossovers slowly at first, then faster, then finally at top speed while controlling a puck. General characteristics of crossovers can be summarized as follows:

1. Forward and backward crossovers are very similar.

2. The term *crossover* refers to the passing of the outside skate (the one nearer the outside of the curve) in front of the toe of the inside skate (figure 6.1).

3. Crossovers are *always* skated on edges: therefore, the line of travel is *always* a curve. The manner in which the skates and body coordinate to produce edges for crossovers (figure 6.2) is discussed in chapter 1.

Figure 6.1 Crossovers: Outside foot crosses over the toe of the inside foot.

Figure 6.2 Skates and body coordinate to produce edges for crossovers.

4. Crossovers require strong, simultaneous edging with both the pushing and gliding skates. On both forward and backward crossovers the inside foot *always* glides on its outside edge, while the outside foot *always* glides on its inside edge.

5. The skates and knees lean into the curve at strong angles. Deeper edges and higher speeds produce sharper curves.

6. As in all skating maneuvers power is achieved by employing the principles of wind-up, release, follow-through, and return. Review the principles of edges, knee bend, body weight, weight shift, and glide, and apply them to crossovers as described in the following list:

   • Each thrust begins with the pushing skate under the center of gravity and finishes with the pushing leg fully extended away from the body.

   • Strong edges are required for the pushing skate to grip the ice and for the gliding skate to skate a curved path.

   • In order to push, knees must be bent deeply (approximately 90 degrees) with body weight concentrated over the thrusting skate.

   • Body weight transfers from pushing skate to gliding skate at the midpoint of each push.

   • The knee of the gliding leg stays well bent as the pushing leg thrusts to full extension and as the pushing leg returns.

   • Each leg, after reaching full extension, returns quickly to a position under the center of gravity to prepare for the next thrust.

   • The returning skate stays within an inch of the ice as it returns.

7. The combination of powerful, complete leg drive and rapid leg movement produces speed. *One without the other is insufficient.*

Forward Crossovers

These instructions are for skating on a counterclockwise circle. The left leg is the inside leg. The right leg is the outside leg. Crossovers in the counterclockwise direction are referred to as right-over-left crossovers.

The First Push: The Stride Push

I call this the *stride push* because it is essentially the same as the push of the forward stride. The stride push is always executed with the outside leg and the push is always against the inside edge.

1. Prepare to glide forward on the outside edge of the inside skate (LFO) and to push against the inside edge of the outside skate.

Wind-Up

2. Place your weight over the outside skate, bend your knees deeply, and dig the inside edge of the outside skate into the ice so that the skate and lower leg form a 45-degree angle to the ice.

Release

3. Push directly back and out against the entire length of the inside edge (figure 6.3a). Do not push the leg straight back in a walking or running motion as this will cause a slip against the flat of the blade rather than a push against the edge.

a   b

c   d

e   f

Figure 6.3 Forward crossover sequence: *(a-c)* stride push; *(d)* return of outside skate; *(e-f)* X push.

Follow-Through

4. Start the push with the heel of the inside edge, shifting your weight forward on the blade as you push; complete the push with the toe flick (front of the inside edge), as you would on the thrust of the forward stride. Be sure to thrust to full extension.

5. At the midpoint of the push, transfer your weight from the inside edge of the right skate onto the outside edge of the left skate (LFO; figure 6.3b). The LFO takes the ice approximately three-quarters of a blade length forward of where the right skate had been gliding on the ice before the first push.* Glide on the LFO, with the left knee well bent throughout the glide.

6. At the finish of the push, the knee of the pushing leg (now the free leg) must lock, with that skate about one inch from and almost parallel to the ice. The toe should be slightly closer to the ice than the heel (figure 6.3c). The knee of the gliding (left) leg maintains a strong 90-degree knee bend.

Return

7. Immediately after the pushing (right) leg locks, return it quickly and move it forward. Prepare to cross it in front of the toe of the gliding skate (figure 6.3d).

8. Keep the right skate close and almost parallel to the ice as it moves forward and crosses over in front of the left skate.

9. The right skate takes your weight and becomes the gliding skate at the midpoint of the second push. It takes the ice on the RFI slightly forward of where the left skate had originally been gliding prior to pushing (figure 6.3e). Leave at least an inch of space between the heel of the right skate and the toe of the left skate while crossing over. This will prevent your feet from hitting each other or getting tangled up during the crossover.

10. Maintain a deep knee bend on the right knee as the RFI takes the ice.

The Second Push: The X Push

I call this the X *push* or *scissor push* because of the X or scissor-like motion created by one leg crossing under the body to push while the other leg crosses over to take the ice and glide. This push is always executed with the outside edge of the inside leg. The X push is sometimes called a *cross-under push* because it actually crosses (drives) *under* the body to generate.

---

* On all skating strides the directional (glide) skate must move slightly ahead of the pushing skate (there is a progression of movement) before it takes the ice. It takes the ice ahead of the pushing skate—forward if skating forward, or backward if skating backward—by approximately three-quarters of a blade length.

Imagine using your legs to create the letter X. To create an X, one leg moves one way (let's say to the right) to cross over the other while the other leg moves the other way (in this case, to the left) to cross under the other. *Both legs* must actively move in opposite directions to complete this motion. Think of it as an over-under motion of the legs.

1. Before the right skate takes the ice to glide on the RFI, the left leg initiates the second push. Until now you have been gliding on the LFO.

Wind-Up

2. Deepen the LFO by increasing the pressure against the outside of the skate and by bending your knees. Keep your weight over the LFO (figure 6.3d).

Release

3. Thrust the left leg underneath your body, directly back and out against the entire length of the outside edge (figure 6.3e).

Follow-Through

4. Push to full extension. Start the push with the heel of the outside edge, shift your weight forward on the blade as you push, and complete the push with the toe flick (front of the outside edge) (figure 6.3f).

Note: Do not push the leg straight back in a walking or running motion as this will cause a slip against the flat of the blade rather than a push against the edge.

Note: Avoid pointing the toe down and heel up; this will cause the front tip of the skate to catch the ice and your skate will slip backward, disengaging the outside edge, eliminating the thrust, and possibly causing a fall (figure 6.4).

5. At the midpoint of the X push, transfer your weight from the LFO onto the RFI, which now becomes the gliding skate.
6. Thrust until the left leg reaches full extension outside the circle (figure 6.3f). At the finish of the push, the knee of the pushing leg—now the free leg—should

Figure 6.4 Incorrect X push. Skate slips back.

Figure 6.5 Return—correct.

be locked, with the free skate held about one inch from and almost parallel with the ice, though the toe will be slightly closer to the ice than the heel. The knee of the gliding skate should still be deeply bent.

Return

7. Immediately after locking the pushing (left) leg, bring it quickly back to center under your body, in a side-by-side position with the gliding skate.

8. Keep the left skate close to and almost parallel with the ice as it returns (figure 6.5). Lifting it high off the ice raises the center of gravity and delays the return process.

You have completed one sequence of the forward crossover. Continue the crossover sequence by thrusting the right leg against the inside edge of the right skate and gliding onto the LFO.

Skating Clockwise

Mirror the procedure for skating counterclockwise. The right skate is now the inside skate, and the left skate is now the outside skate. You will now be doing left over right crossovers.

Points to Remember for Forward Crossovers

• The one-third, one-third, one-third principle of the forward stride also applies to both pushes of forward crossovers.

• When gliding on the outside edge of the inside skate, keep your body weight on the back half of the blade. If your weight is too far forward, the outside edge cannot cut into the ice; the skate will fishtail into a skid, causing a loss of grip against the ice and a subsequent loss of balance. Even a deeply edged skate will skid if the body weight is too far forward above the outside edge. The tighter the curve and the faster you're traveling, the more you must concentrate your weight on the back half of the outside edge.

• Keep the entire blade length of each gliding skate in complete contact with the ice. You will lose your balance if you glide on just the toe.

• When quick acceleration is needed, run the first one or two crossover sequences on the toes (fronts of the edges). However, even while running the crossovers, stay low and project your weight in the direction of travel. Thrust against the edges with powerful and full leg drive. Small hopping steps take you nowhere fast; jumping upward destroys forward momentum.

• The process of crossing the inside leg under the body to push is much more pronounced than the process of crossing the outside skate over the inside skate to glide.

Note: Remember that on all skating strides the directional skate must move ahead of the previous skate in the desired direction of travel—forward if skating forward, or backward if skating backward—by approximately three-quarters of a blade length.

Backward Crossovers

Backward crossovers are important for every player's maneuverability but are especially critical in defensive situations. Defenders use them to track opponents and to take opponents out of the play (for example, in a backward-to-forward turn when racing to cut off an attacking player at the boards).

It is important to understand when it's appropriate to use backward crossovers and when it isn't. A good rule is to use backward crossovers when there is plenty of distance between the forward and the defender. When the forward is bearing down on the defender, the defender should *not* cross over because this can create an opportunity for the forward to cut the other way and escape from the defender.

Defenders must always face the action and the opposition. This means they must be able to start out backward quickly and explosively. Players who can't are forced to start out forward, take a couple of strides, and then turn around backward. For those few strides they are unaware of the action behind their backs. Thus they break one of the cardinal rules in hockey: never turn your back to the play. Backward crossovers are the fastest and most effective way of accelerating backward while still being able to see the action.

When skated counterclockwise, the backward crossover is a left-skate-over-right-skate maneuver. The right skate is the inside skate (nearer the inside of the curve), and the left skate is the outside skate (nearer the outside of the curve). As in forward crossovers, the outside skate always crosses in front of the toe of the inside skate (figure 6.6) while the inside leg crosses (drives) under the body to push.

The instructions given here are for skating on a counterclockwise circle.

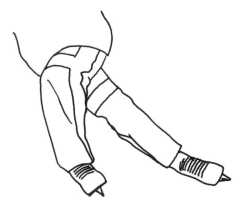

Figure 6.6 Backward crossover: left over right.

The First Push: The Stride Push

Because the stride push of the backward stride is the C-cut, the stride push of the backward crossover is the C-cut. It is always executed with the outside leg. However, on its return, instead of centering under the body as it would on the backward stride, the returning C-cut skate crosses over in front of the toe of the gliding skate.

1. Prepare to glide backward on the outside edge of the inside skate (RBO) and to push with the inside edge of the outside leg.

Wind-Up

2. Place your weight over the outside (left) skate, bend your knees deeply, and dig the inside edge into the ice so the skate and lower leg form a 45-degree angle to the ice.

Release

3. Pivot the left heel outward (toward the outside of the circle), and execute a C-cut push against the inside edge of the left skate (figure 6.7a). Thrust the left leg to the front and side, pushing directly against the entire blade length of the inside edge.

4. At the midpoint of the push, transfer your weight from the inside edge of the left skate (LBI) to the outside edge of the right skate (RBO). Keep the right knee well bent throughout the glide (figure 6.7b).

Follow-Through

5. Thrust to full extension. At the end of the thrust the pushing leg (now the free leg) should be locked, with that skate held close to or even on the ice.

6. Immediately after locking the pushing (left) leg, return it quickly and begin to cross it over in front of the toe of the right skate. Keep it close to (or on) the ice as it moves to cross over (see figure 6.7b). While

a   b   c

Figure 6.7 Backward crossover sequence (counterclockwise).

crossing the left skate over, leave at least an inch of space between its heel and the toe of the right skate. In this way your feet won't get tangled.

7. At the midpoint of the second push, transfer your weight onto the left inside edge, which now becomes the gliding skate. Keep the left knee well bent throughout the glide.

The Second Push: The X Push

This push is always executed with the inside leg. It is identical to the X (scissor) push for forward crossovers.

Before the left skate takes the ice to glide on its inside edge, the inside leg, the skate of which has been gliding on its outside edge, must be activated to provide the second thrust. As always, the wind-up is required for power.

Wind-Up

1. Deepen the RBO by increasing the pressure against the outside of the boot, bending your knees, and placing your weight over the RBO.

Release

2. Thrust the right leg sideways underneath your body directly forward and outward against the entire outside edge (figure 6.7c).

Follow-Through

3. Start the push with the middle of the outside edge, shift your weight forward on the blade as you push, and complete the push with the toe flick from the front of the outside edge.

Do not push the leg in a straight back (walking or running) motion, as this will cause a slip against the flat of the blade rather than a push against the edge. As in forward crossovers, avoid pointing the toe straight down and the heel up as this will cause a slip against the ice and a resultant loss of balance and power.

4. At the midpoint of the push, transfer your weight from the RBO to the LBI, which takes the ice as the gliding skate (figure 6.7c).

5. Continue to thrust with the right leg until it reaches full extension outside the circle. At the end of the thrust the knee of the pushing leg—now the free leg—should be locked, with the free skate held close to and almost parallel with the ice, though the toe will be slightly closer to the ice than the heel. The knee of the gliding leg should, of course, remain deeply bent (figure 6.7c).

Return

6. Immediately after the right leg locks, bring it quickly back to its return position under the midpoint of your body. Keep it close to and almost parallel with the ice as it returns.

You have finished one sequence. Repeat the procedure, pivoting the left skate outward to execute the C-cut push against the inside edge of the left skate and gliding on the RBO.

Skating Clockwise

Mirror the procedure just described. The left skate is the inside skate, and the right skate is the outside skate (figure 6.8, a-c). You will be doing right over left crossovers.

Remember: On all skating strides the directional skate must move ahead of the previous skate in the desired direction of travel—forward if skating forward or backward if skating backward—by approximately three-quarters of a blade length. Be sure to place each gliding skate slightly ahead (behind you, when skating backward) of where the previous skate was gliding before it pushed.

c　　　　　　　　　　b　　　　　　　　　　a

Figure 6.8 Backward crossover sequence (clockwise).

Stride Tempos

As in forward and backward striding, all stride lengths and stride tempos must be equal. A stride in which one leg pushes fully and the other pushes only partially is insufficient. The same is true of a stride in which one leg moves rapidly and the other moves slowly.

Try to develop varying rhythms on forward and backward crossovers. Remember that all strides should be full strides and that stride tempo depends on how quickly the free leg returns to its position under the center of gravity so that you can change feet. Practice correctly and slowly, then correctly faster, fastest, and even at speeds that put you out of control (over-speed training); first without, then while controlling a puck.

Points to Remember for Forward and Backward Crossovers

• The crossover sequence includes two pushes—the first from the inside edge of the outside skate, the second from the outside edge of the inside skate. If one is eliminated, you lose half your power.

• The depth of the edges applied to the ice is directly related to speed and to the sharpness of the curve. Use shallower edges when traveling slowly on a large curve than when traveling fast on a sharp curve. Develop the ability to adjust the depth of your edges to the situation at hand: sharper curves and greater speed require greater lean of edges and knees.

• The manner in which the skate and body coordinate to produce curves, as explained in chapter 1, should be carefully reviewed.

• It is always the outside skate that crosses over in front of the toe of the inside skate.

• The quality of the X (scissor) push affects the quality of the crossover maneuver. If this push is only partially used, power is lost and the crossover itself is incomplete. When the scissoring action is executed properly, the legs cross at the tops of the thighs, not just at the knees.

• The process of crossing the inside leg under the body to push is more pronounced than the process of crossing the outside leg over in front of the inside leg.

• The ability of goalies to perform forward and backward crossovers depends on a complete scissoring action. The X push driving fully under the body creates room for the outside leg to cross over beyond the bulky pads.

• Keep the free skate close to and almost parallel with the ice after each thrust and during each return. Feel as if you are dragging the skate on the ice as it returns. Kicking up the heels (caused by pointing the toe down) or lifting the skate high off the ice (caused by excessively flexing the knee of the free leg) delays the return process and raises the center of gravity.

• When performing forward or backward crossovers keep the skates parallel to each other and facing along the line of travel. If either skate turns at an angle different from the line of travel, the line of travel will change. You might end up with your skates sliding sideways into a skid.

Points to Remember for Backward Crossovers

- For additional speed on backward crossovers: Simultaneously with the first push (the C-cut push) and while the inside skate is still off the ice, reach the inside skate and leg sideways into the circle. When the inside skate takes the ice, your feet should be somewhat wider apart than your shoulders (figure 6.9a). This allows for a more complete C-cut thrust.

- Execute the backward X push as if the inside skate and leg were scooping the circle (pulling the ice) under you (figure 6.9b).

- Drive the inside leg well underneath your body *before* attempting to cross the outside leg over. If you don't use this sequence, your skates might get tangled up as you attempt to cross the outside leg over.

a   **b**

Figure 6.9 *(a)* Inside skate reaches into the circle; *(b)* inside skate and leg "scoop circle" under the body.

- Keep your body weight over the front halves of the blades but be sure the entire blade lengths (not just the toes) of both skates are on the ice.

- Crossing the inside leg under the body to push is more pronounced than crossing the outside leg over in front of the inside skate.

- Keep hips and feet facing directly backward over the line of travel. There is a tendency to turn the hips sideways as you cut the C. This will force you to skate sideways instead of backward.

- Good posture is critical. If you lean too far forward, your weight will pitch over the toes of your blades, with a resultant loss of balance. If you need to lean on your stick for balance, your body weight is too far forward. Keep your weight concentrated over the front halves of the blades.

Backward crossovers differ from forward crossovers in the following ways:

- As in all backward skating, your body weight is over the front halves of the blades.
- When executing right-over-left backward crossovers, you travel a clockwise curve. The inside skate is the left skate, and the outside skate is the right skate. Left-over-right backward crossovers are just the opposite.
- The push from the inside edge is the C-cut push, as in straight backward skating, and the thrust is to the front and side.
- The returning (free) skate may actually stay in slight contact with the ice rather than coming off it.

Body Position and Control in Crossovers

The ability to maneuver while skating on a curve or circle is affected by the position and control of your upper body. The hips and skates always face the direction of travel. Shoulders remain still and level with the ice. Excessive arm, chest, shoulder, and head movement affects balance, agility, and maneuverability (BAM), as well as the ability to control the puck.

Two upper-body positions may be used when performing forward crossovers, and both must be mastered: (a) chest and shoulders face toward the center of the curve or circle (figure 6.10a); (b) chest and shoulders face toward the outside of the curve or circle (figure 6.10b). In both positions the upper body (from the waist to the shoulders) twists about a quarter turn in opposition to the hips, which *always* face the direction of travel. This twisting of the upper body is called *torque;* it is essential to torque the upper body when skating on curves or circles.

a   b

Figure 6.10 Body positions for forward crossovers: Upper body faces: *(a)* toward center of curve, or *(b)* away from center of curve.

Only one upper-body position is generally used for backward crossovers; this is position *a* (chest and shoulders facing into the curve).

Shoulders should be level with the ice. *Leaning* is accomplished by leaning the skates, knees, and hips (lower body) into the circle. If you lean or tilt your upper body into the circle by dropping the inside shoulder, you can easily fall or be knocked down.

Practice crossovers while holding the hockey stick with both hands. Keep the stick on the ice in its correct position for controlling a puck while skating on circles. Practice on both forehand and backhand sides. Practice both body positions with forward crossovers and position *a* with backward crossovers.

Practice crossovers holding the hockey stick with just your top hand. Then practice crossovers in this way while keeping the puck on the stick as you skate. Keep your arms, chest, and shoulders still as you perform crossovers. Excessive movement will cause you to lose the puck.

Mats Sundin in excellent position for skating crossovers with his chest facing out of the curve.

Exercises for Improving Forward and Backward Crossovers

The exercises in this section help develop

- proper use of the edges,
- power on both pushes, and
- correct body position and control.

Practice all exercises equally in the clockwise and counterclockwise directions.

Walking Crossovers

This is an effective exercise to learn the basic steps of the crossover sequence (both forward and backward). Keep both skates facing the same goal line throughout, and practice it crossing over in both directions.

Stand at one sideboards of the rink facing the goal line. Perform walking crossovers across the ice to the opposite sideboards. Walk to the left, always crossing the right skate over the left. The right (outside or trailing) skate pushes against its inside edge (stride push) as the left (inside or leading) skate steps onto its outside edge. After pushing with the right leg, cross the right skate over in front of the left skate and land on the right inside edge while the left leg crosses under the body to push (X push). Keep both skates pointing at the goal line. Do walking crossovers in this manner from one set of sideboards to the other.

Variation

Do the same exercise, now pushing the legs sideways to full extension on each push. This helps develop the ability to feel both the direction and extension of the leg drive from the stride and X pushes.

Outside Edge X or Scissor Cuts

The purpose of this exercise is to practice outside edge thrusts. Both the gliding and thrusting skates must be on *outside* edges at all times. Note the scissoring action of the legs as one crosses under the body to push and the other crosses over to glide.

1. Skate forward on the LFO, right foot off the ice. You will curve in a counterclockwise direction (figure 6.11a).
2. Begin to cross the right skate over the left.
3. Thrust the left leg against its outside edge as the right skate crosses over. Thrust the left leg sideways underneath your body to full extension.

4. The right skate, after crossing over, should take the ice on its RFO to glide on a clockwise curve (figure 6.11b).

5. Lift the left skate off the ice (figure 6.11c). Uncross it. Bring it forward and alongside the right skate in preparation for crossing it in front of the right skate (figure 6.11d). As the left skate uncrosses and moves forward, keep it close to and parallel with the ice.

6. Prepare to push with the right leg as the left skate moves forward.

7. Thrust the right leg against its outside edge as the left skate crosses over. Thrust it sideways underneath your body to full extension. The left skate, after crossing over, will take the ice on its LFO to glide on a counterclockwise curve (figure 6.11e).

8. You have completed one sequence. Keep repeating the sequence, continuously crossing over and thrusting under.

9. Perform the same skating exercise backward (figure 6.11, e-a).

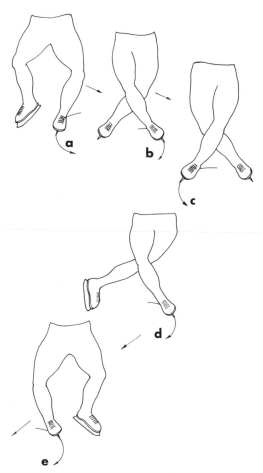

Figure 6.11 Outside edge scissor cuts, alternating feet.

Points to Remember

- Glide on and push from outside edges.
- Glide on and push against the entire blade lengths.
- Push to full extension.

Note: Start this exercise slowly. Try to accelerate with each successive thrust. It is not sufficient to merely maintain speed with each thrust. Pushing involves gaining speed. If you don't increase speed with each push, you are not thrusting correctly or with optimum force.

Note: After completing six pushes, come to a complete stop and begin the exercise again. Start slowly and try to build speed with each thrust.

S-Cuts

This exercise involves executing a series of S-cuts into the ice. It is performed on one skate at a time. The drill is difficult, but it will help you master inside and outside edges, both of which are essential for skating curves and circles. It is also excellent for developing balance, knee bend, and strong quadriceps.

S-cuts are created by alternately cutting a small semicircle into the ice with the RFO (clockwise) and then with the RFI (counterclockwise), and repeating the sequence continuously (figure 6.12).

1. Glide forward on a deep RFO. Keep the left skate off the ice and next to the right skate.

2. Bend the right knee deeply, flip the right ankle inward, and shift your weight so the skate is now on its inside edge, thereby changing the outside-edge lean of the skate to an inside-edge lean (45 degrees) of the skate. You will now be skating on the RFI.

3. While on the RFI, slightly straighten your right knee to release your weight. Then, to change to the right outside edge, bend the right knee deeply while flipping the ankle outward and shifting your weight so that you once again skate on the RFO. Keep your weight on the back half of the blade as you bend your knee.

4. While bending your knee deeply and keeping your weight on the back half of the blade, attempt to make the edge *cut* a semicircle into the ice. When executed properly, the cut accelerates you forward.

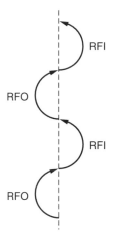

Figure 6.12 Forward S cuts on right foot: An imaginary axis divides the outside edge curve from the inside edge curve.

5. See how many S-cuts you can execute before having to put the left skate down.

6. Try to skate the entire length of the ice on the right skate, accelerating on each edge.

7. Repeat the exercise on the left skate.

8. Repeat the exercise skating backward on each skate, now keeping your weight on the front halves of the edges. Again, only one skate should be on the ice for each set of S-cuts.

Coaching Tip

It is easier to cut into the ice with the inside edge than it is with the outside edge. Try to develop the ability to cut equally with outside and inside edges so that the depth of each cut is the same.

---

9. Strong edge angles and a strong rise and fall of the skating knee are needed to perform this drill properly.

10. A long-term goal for advanced players should be to perform one set of S-cuts on each skate (forward and backward) for an entire lap of the rink.

Note: Body weight must be on the back half of the blade when performing this move forward, and on the front half when performing it backward.

Resistance Crossovers

The purpose of this exercise is to develop correct and powerful leg drive on forward and backward crossovers. It involves pushing a resisting player while executing crossovers.

Stand sideways to another player, holding a hockey stick horizontally at chest height between you. Prepare to push the resisting player, who should face you and be positioned to glide backward.

Move the resisting player by executing a series of crossovers. The resisting player should prevent you from moving too easily by putting on the brakes with a two-foot backward snowplow stop (see chapter 8, pages 138 and 139).

To move the resisting player you must dig the edges strongly into the ice and thrust powerfully with each leg. You actually will be doing walking crossovers across the ice. The leading skate corresponds to the inside skate on crossovers; it steps onto and thrusts against its outside edge. The trailing skate corresponds to the outside skate; it thrusts against its inside edge, crosses over in front of the toe of the inside leg, and steps down onto its inside edge.

Thrust to full extension on every push. Keep your head up and shoulders back as you push the resisting player across the ice. Push the player all the way across the ice doing right-over-left crossovers (figure 6.13, a-d). Coming back, use left-over-right crossovers. As always, practice both sides equally.

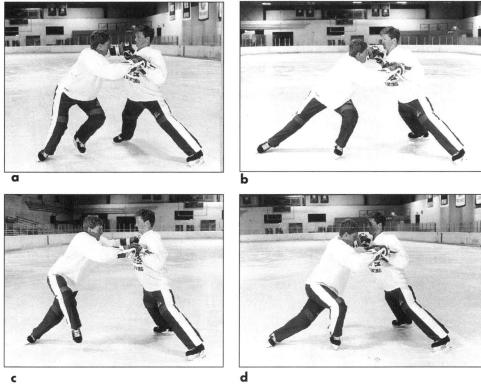

Figure 6.13 Resistance crossovers.

C-Cuts on a Circle

1. This exercise improves the outside leg thrust of the crossover sequence while training the inside skate to glide on its outside edge. Skate around a face-off circle in a clockwise direction. The inside skate should continuously glide on its outside edge. Thrust continuously with the inside edge of the outside (left) leg by executing consecutive C-cuts around the circle (figure 6.14). Be sure

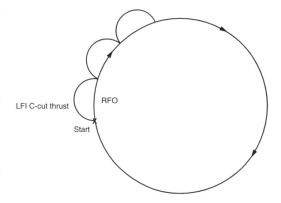

Figure 6.14 Forward C-cuts on a circle: clockwise direction.

to bring the pushing leg completely back under your body on the return phase of each C-cut. Maintain a deep knee bend on the glide leg throughout. No bobbing up and down.

2. Repeat the exercise skating around the face-off circle in a counterclockwise direction.

3. Repeat the exercise skating backward around a face-off circle (both directions).

Crossovers on a Circle

When practicing crossovers on a circle, it is good practice to hold the hockey stick with both hands and to keep the stick on the ice in a position that allows you to maintain control of a puck at all times. With forward crossovers you can use either upper-body position: chest facing into or out of the circle. Keep your shoulders from moving while skating crossovers. You can't control a puck if your chest and shoulders move excessively because every movement of the upper body causes a corresponding movement of the stick.

As you gain upper-body control, practice holding the hockey stick with just the top hand. Again, prevent your shoulders from moving. Now perform this exercise with a puck. First, hold the hockey stick with two hands, then with one hand.

Perform the same exercise skating backward crossovers using the upper-body position with chest and shoulders facing into the center of the circle.

Consecutive Crossovers

Skate consecutive crossovers on a face-off circle. Learning skaters should focus on applying the edges as discussed previously. More advanced skaters should use very strong edges and deep knee bend, and make the circle as tight as possible while skating as fast as possible. Do not lean the inside shoulder into the circle; this will cause upper-body tilt into the circle and a serious loss of balance, especially at high speeds.

Note: When skating in the direction that has you holding the hockey stick on your backhand side (bottom hand across your body), it is difficult to eliminate all lean of the shoulders into the circle. Try to minimize it.

Variation

Vary this drill by skating the circle three times using forward crossovers, then turning backward and skating the circle three times using backward crossovers.

Freeze Drill

Perform consecutive crossovers on a face-off circle, skating fast. On a whistle signal, freeze so that you are balanced on whichever edge you happen to be gliding on when the whistle is blown; keep the other skate off the ice. See how long you can balance (freeze your weight) on that edge without putting the other skate down. Do this on both outside and inside edges in both directions, using forward and backward crossovers. This is a test of your balance on each edge at any given moment.

Five-Circle Crossovers

Start from one corner of the rink. Skate around the nearest face-off circle one time, using forward or backward crossovers. Then skate to the next face-off circle, and skate crossovers around it one full time in the other direction. Skate to the next circle, and skate around it one full time in the original direction. Continue until you have skated around all five face-off circles (figure 6.15).

Alternate the direction of crossovers on each circle. Pay attention to improving the more difficult direction. Use proper technique. Go slowly at first; think about and feel what you're doing and try to correct errors. As technique improves, accelerate the pace until you can perform correct technique at increasingly faster speeds.

Incorporate the puck with both forward and backward crossovers. Practice both upper-body positions when skating forward. When skating around the circles alternate holding the hockey stick with two hands and one hand. When striding forward or backward from circle to circle, hold the stick with just the top hand using the correct arm swing of the forward and backward stride.

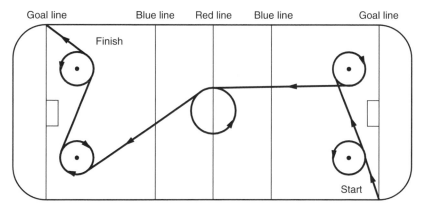

Figure 6.15 Five-circle crossovers.

Variations on Crossover Exercises

There are numerous variations on crossover exercises. These are just a sampling and may be expanded or changed.

Crossovers in Figure-Eight Patterns

1. Skate consecutive crossovers on a circle, clockwise. After skating around the circle twice, skate to a second, tangential circle and skate around it twice, counterclockwise. Then skate to the original circle and skate crossovers around it, clockwise. Keep repeating.

2. Skate forward crossovers on a circle two times, then skate to the second circle and do backward crossovers two times around. Return to the original circle and skate forward crossovers two times around. Keep repeating.

3. Repeat crossovers as outlined in steps 1 and 2, but this time with the puck and using both upper-body positions.

Crossovers on the Same Circle

1. Skate crossovers two times on a face-off circle, clockwise. At the blowing of a whistle, stop, change direction, and skate crossovers two times on the same circle, counterclockwise.

2. Skate forward crossovers two times on a face-off circle, then turn and skate backward crossovers two times on the same circle. Be sure to practice both directions.

3. Incorporate the puck and practice skating with the puck using both upper-body positions.

C-Cut Crossovers

This exercise involves skating forward crossovers on a circle, but in this variation of crossovers the heels of both skates must stay *on the ice* at all times. The edges used for gliding and pushing are the same as in regular crossovers. Both pushes (from the outside leg and from the inside leg) are executed solely with the back halves of the blades. *The toes are not used.* The directions given apply to skating on a counterclockwise circle.

The First Push

This is a C-cut push against the inside edge.

1. Use the inside edge of the outside (right) skate to execute a forward C-cut push.

2. Push with the back half of the blade. Keep the heel of the skate on the ice as the leg pushes and reaches full extension (figure 6.16a).

3. During the push, shift your weight onto, and glide on, the LFO.

4. Keep the right heel on the ice as you bring the right skate forward to cross over in front of the toe of your left skate.

The Second Push

This is a C-cut push against the outside edge.

1. Thrust the inside (left) leg against its outside edge (crossing it under your body), forming a reverse C-cut (figure 6.16b).

2. Push with the back half of the blade. Keep the heel of the skate on the ice as the leg pushes and reaches full extension.

3. During the push, shift your weight onto, and glide on, the RFI.

4. After the left leg reaches full extension under your body (simulating the X push), keep the left heel on the ice and glide the left skate back to a position alongside your right skate. You have completed one sequence.

a   b

Figure 6.16   C-cut crossovers: *(a)* C-cut push, *(b)* X push.

Keep repeating the sequence. Then mirror these instructions and practice skating on a clockwise circle. The exercise can also be done using backward crossovers, but because of its difficulty this is recommended for more advanced skaters.

Forward C-cut crossovers develop many of the skills needed for effective crossover strides:

• Maintaining a strong knee bend on the gliding skate during the actual crossover move

- Keeping the body weight on the pushing leg for an effective push
- Using the back half of the blade to initiate each push (front half when skating this exercise backward)
- Developing powerful leg drive
- Developing full extension
- Training the return skate to stay close to and parallel with the ice as it moves back to its original position under the body

Body Control Exercises

These exercises stress correct upper-body position and control. Position your upper body properly and control excessive arm, shoulder, and chest movement, and you will be a better balanced and stronger skater. Some professional hockey players who are not exceptionally fast compensate for having less speed by having superb balance and control.

Crossovers: Chest Facing Into the Circle

Skate the following exercises with your chest facing the center of the circle. The object is to train the upper body to remain still while performing forward and backward crossovers.

1. Skate crossovers on a circle. Hold a hockey stick with both hands, keeping the stick blade on the ice. If your chest and shoulders are positioned properly, the stick should ride inside the circle and the tip of the stick blade should point toward the face-off dot at the center of the circle. This is the case on both the forehand and backhand sides.

Do not let the stick move around. If you can keep the stick in the same position as you skate, this indicates that your arms, chest, and shoulders are under control. Remember, if you move your arms, chest, and shoulders when carrying a puck, you also are forced to move the hockey stick, which will cause you to lose the puck. It is critical to learn to skate with the upper body unmoving and under control.

2. Skate crossovers with each hockey glove balanced atop each outstretched hand. This requires you to keep arms, chest, and shoulders still; if you move them, the gloves will fall.

3. Skate crossovers holding a cup of water in each outstretched hand. Try not to spill the water. This requires you to hold your upper body, arms, and hands extremely still and under control.

4. Skate crossovers with your hands clasped behind your back, or with your hands on your hips. This prevents arm, chest, and shoulder movement. Practice this using both upper-body positions.

5. A group of about six players forms a circle that is joined by the hockey sticks of each player. Extend your right arm in front of you while holding the top of your hockey stick, and at the same time extend your left arm behind you and grasp the stick blade of the player behind you. Each player's chest should face the center of the circle. When skating forward crossovers around the circle, the direction is counterclockwise; when skating backward crossovers, clockwise.

To do this exercise in the opposite direction, players will extend their left arms out front and their right arms behind them. Linking up in this manner locks the shoulders and chest in the desired upper-body positions. This exercise trains you to keep the upper body in the correct position for skating crossovers.

6. Practice crossovers by yourself, maintaining this body position, holding the hockey stick with just your top hand and keeping the stick in its proper place on the ice as you skate. Do not let it move around. Also, practice while carrying a puck on the stick.

Crossovers: Chest Facing Outside the Circle

This body position is often needed when an attacking player tries to protect the puck while swerving around a defending player. To ward off the defender with the inside arm and shoulder, the attacker's chest must face out of the curve. In game situations attacking players often hold the hockey stick with just their top hand, which helps them to protect the puck.

Skate the following exercises (forward crossovers only) with your back facing the center of the circle. Again, the idea is to train the upper body to remain unmoving and correctly positioned while performing crossovers.

1. Skate forward crossovers on a circle. Hold the hockey stick with both hands, keeping the stick blade on the ice. In this exercise, the stick will be outside the circle. Keep the stick in the same position, without moving it, as you skate around the circles.

2. Perform steps 2, 3, and 4 from the previous set of exercises ("Crossovers: Chest Facing Into the Circle") but now with the chest and shoulders facing outside the circle.

3. A group of about six players should form a circle that is joined by the hockey sticks of each player, as in step 5 of the previous exercise, but now holding the sticks so that chests face outside the circle. For forward crossovers around a counterclockwise circle, the left hand extends to hold the top of the stick in front, and the right hand extends to hold the stick blade of the person in back. Again, the goal is to position the shoulders and chests correctly, to feel the correct upper-body position and to eliminate excessive arm, chest, and shoulder movement.

4. Practice forward crossovers using this upper-body position, now holding the hockey stick with only your top hand. Again, keep the hockey stick in its proper place on the ice as you skate without moving it around. Now practice this while controlling a puck.

Running Crossovers

Figure 6.17 Running crossovers.

When instant acceleration is imperative, players often run or leap the first few strides. These running or leaping strides are very effective when performed correctly.

Practice running crossovers by sprinting on the edges. Don't forget to use the full thrusting action of the legs even when running. Be sure to leap outward, not upward (figure 6.17).

Note: When running, the body weight should be on the toes (fronts of the edges) similar to when starting (see chapter 7). The *toe* is the area from the ball of the foot to the toe.

Skate crossovers on a circle at a slow pace. On a whistle signal, run the crossovers, accelerating with powerful, rapid, and fully extended thrusts. On the next whistle, slow down and use normal crossover strides. On the next, run again. Perform the exercise forward and backward.

Weaving Crossovers for Lateral Mobility

Weaving creates lateral mobility and is accomplished by crossing over one way (right over left) and then alternating to cross over the other way (left over right). In weaving crossovers a third step must be added to the crossover sequence to neutralize the feet, the original direction of curve, and body weight. Only after the neutralizing step can you skate in the new direction.

Weaving crossovers require a sequence of three steps instead of two. It is imperative to gain speed on the third step as well as on the first two steps.

The third push is done with the same leg that did the first push. The push is against the inside edge of the blade and is identical to the first push.

The third step lands on the skate that would be the inside skate (the skate that ordinarily would glide on the outside edge) on a regular crossover, but in this move it (the inside skate) glides on its *inside edge* instead.

The third step is executed as a wide step, planted on a strong inside edge, with the body weight totally committed over the planted (skating) foot. Planting a strong inside edge allows the player to make a quick transition from one direction to another.

Note: Contrary to forward or backward striding, the ability to move sideways is enhanced by maintaining a wide base. In order to shift weight rapidly from side to side, the feet should be somewhat wider apart than the shoulders. Figure 6.18 (a-g) shows a sequence of weaving forward crossovers (lateral mobility). Figure 6.19 (a-h) shows a sequence of weaving backward crossovers.

Figure 6.18 Weaving forward crossover sequence.

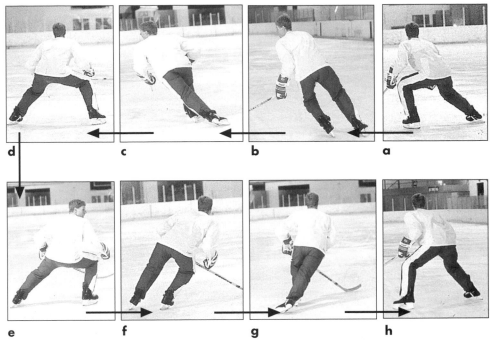

Figure 6.19 Weaving backward crossover sequence.

Figure 6.20 diagrams the pattern of weaving backward crossovers.

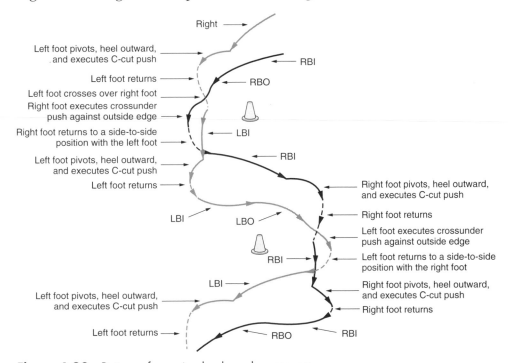

Figure 6.20 Pattern of weaving backward crossovers.

1. Practice weaving crossovers around pylons. Develop the ability to skate a tight S-curve pattern (figure 6.21a).

2. Vary the drill. Skate forward crossovers in an S pattern around two pylons. Then turn around and do the same thing while skating backward crossovers. Figure 6.21b shows a slightly different, more difficult course.

3. Work with another skater, one of you skating as a forward and the other as a defender. The forward, skating with a puck, starts at the goal line and skates forward crossovers weaving laterally down the ice. The defender starts at the first blue line and skates a similar pattern of backward crossovers, trying to track and prevent the forward from passing the defender.

4. Practice lateral mobility down the ice. Skate two crossovers, right over left, and then alternate and do two crossovers, left over right. You can also do these singly or by threes. Do the drill skating forward and backward. Practice stepping out wide and onto the inside edge on the third (neutralizing) step of every sequence.

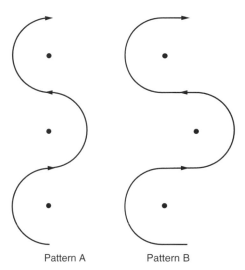

Pattern A   Pattern B

Figure 6.21 Two patterns of weaving crossovers around pylons.

chapter 7

Starts for a Step Advantage on the Opposition

Goals can be scored and hockey games can be won or lost in fractions of a second. The player who gets going fastest is often the one who gets to the puck and gets the advantage. Players who don't start out quickly often end up hopelessly behind the play. Players *must* develop the ability to accelerate explosively from a complete stop, or shift from low to high gear while in motion. Great players can accelerate instantly from any position.

Explosive starts require quick, running-type strides—strides so rapid the player appears to be running rather than skating. These running strides appear choppy because the skates do not glide. They are extremely rapid, but, contrary to popular opinion, they are not short. They are accompanied by extremely powerful and complete leg drive. Explosive acceleration means you have to get somewhere—fast.

The techniques of starting on ice are similar to those of a sprinter leaving the starting block. In both instances the athlete strives for quickness, power, and distance on every thrust.

There are three requirements to achieving explosive acceleration on the ice.

1. Quickness—quick feet, or rapid leg turnover. To achieve quickness, a skater must "run" the first few strides on the toes (fronts of the inside edges) of the skates. The skates move so rapidly that they appear to play touch-and-go with the ice. If the entire blade length contacts the ice, the skate is forced to glide. Gliding takes time and delays the next stride.

2. Power. Power is derived from the force exerted by the legs and body weight driving directly against the gripping edge. Full leg drive and total leg recovery are as imperative when starting as when striding. Nothing can propel you forward unless the legs drive fully in the opposite direction.

3. Distance—outward motion. To achieve distance the body weight must project in the desired direction of travel. The distance covered in the starting strides is distinctly related to the forward angle of the upper body. A strong forward angle of the upper body produces greater distance. Because the skating (contact) foot must take the ice under the center of gravity (midsection), the further forward the upper body is projected, the further forward the foot must step in order to maintain balance. In other words, while running the first few strides, you must also throw your body weight outward. This is similar to a sprinter taking off from the starting block.

There are three basic starts in hockey: *forward*, *side (crossover)*, and *backward*. As in every aspect of skating, the ingredients for explosive starts include

- the proper use of edges to provide grip into the ice,
- proper distribution of body weight, and
- optimum leg thrust and rapid leg motion.

The principles of wind-up, release, follow-through, and return always apply. By developing the three basic starts, you can achieve an explosive takeoff no matter which way you are facing when you stop and no matter in which direction you want to move when you go.

When starting explosively with the puck, it's extremely important to keep the puck out well ahead of you. If the puck is too close to your body you have nowhere to go because the puck blocks your progress. The general rule for accelerating with the puck is that the puck must go first; you follow it.

Front or Forward Start

A *front (forward) start* is used when you are facing straight ahead to where you want to go—for example, if you have skated backward, stopped, and need to skate forward in the direction you came from. Another example is from a face-off—if the puck ends up straight ahead of you, you need to start straight forward from your position on the face-off circle.

The First Stride

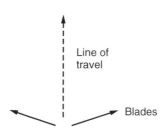

Figure 7.1 Front (forward) start: feet pivoted outward about 80 degrees from line of travel.

This description assumes you are using the right leg as the initial pushing leg.

1. Pivot both skates and knees outward in an exaggerated V-diamond position (heels together, toes apart). Each skate should be turned outward at an angle (approximately 80 to 85 degrees) to the forward line of travel (figures 7.1 and 7.2a).

2. Place your weight over the pushing (right) skate (figure 7.2b).

Wind-Up

3. Bend your knees deeply (90 degrees) and dig the inside edge of the pushing skate into the ice so that the skate and lower leg form a strong (approximately 45-degree) angle to the ice. The stronger the pressure into the ice of edge, knee bend, and body weight, the more power available for the thrust.

4. As you begin to push, shift your body weight strongly forward in the desired direction of travel. Your body weight must be low and angled well forward, prepared for being propelled powerfully by the thrusting skate and leg, which push directly against the cutting edge (figure 7.2c). Because your body weight is angled so far forward the primary thrust is executed with the front portion of the inside edge. As you shift your weight outward, reach forward with the front (left) knee and skate. Keep moving the front skate forward until it makes contact with the ice under your center of gravity (figure 7.2, d-e). Powerful leg drive, the inclination of the upper body, and the reach of the front knee and skate combine to produce forward motion.

5. The front (left) skate should contact the ice on the first two inches of inside edge (45-degree edge angle) with the skate turned outward approximately 70 to 75 degrees from the forward line of travel. The heel of the blade should *not* touch the ice. When the left skate touches down properly—gripping the ice strongly with the inside edge, with your body weight over it—it is immediately prepared to push (figure 7.2e). If it does not touch down on a strong enough edge or if your weight is on the heel of the blade, the skate will be forced to glide. Gliding negatively affects the acceleration process and delays the next stride.

6. After thrusting, the pushing skate and leg (now the free skate and leg) must immediately return, pass by the contact skate (in the V-diamond position) and reach forward to become the new contact skate. Keep the returning knee and skate turned outward as they return, pass the contact skate, and move forward to take the ice (figure 7.2f).

The Second Stride

1. The left skate has taken the ice on the toe of the inside edge with your body weight centered over it, knee well bent. As the left skate contacts the ice, it immediately becomes the new pushing skate.

Note: Landing on the inside edge is imperative to set up the next push.

Thrust powerfully, pushing directly against the inside edge. Keep your body weight low and angled well forward. Push to full extension. As you push, continue to shift your weight forward and reach forward with the right knee and skate, moving the skate forward until it makes contact with the ice under your center of gravity (figure 7.2g).

a

b

c

d

e

f

g

Figure 7.2 Front (forward) start sequence.

2. When the right skate takes the ice, it should touch down on only the toe of the inside edge with the skate still turned outward and your body weight totally over the edge. On this second stride the skate should be turned outward about 60 to 65 degrees from the forward line of travel. Your weight should be only on the front two to three inches of the inside edge. If your weight is on the heel of the blade, the skate will be forced to glide, causing slower leg speed and a resultant delay of the next stride.

3. After thrusting, the left skate and leg (now the free skate and leg) must immediately return, pass by the contact skate (in the V-diamond position) and reach forward to become the new contact skate. Keep the returning knee and skate turned outward as they return, pass the contact skate, and move forward to take the ice.

Subsequent Strides

You have completed the first two running steps of the start. Some players take three or four running steps. The number of running steps is often determined by the specific game situation. For example, if you have a lot of open ice ahead of you, take three or four running steps to escape. In situations where the opponent is pressing, you might be able to take only one or two running steps.

After the running steps your skating motion should become similar to that of the forward stride. In other words, you need to take advantage of the glide of the skate. Continue to move your legs in a rapid sprinting motion. The angle of the upper body to the ice should gradually become more upright. By the fifth or sixth stride it should be in the forward stride position, inclined approximately 45 degrees to the ice. If the upper body becomes upright too suddenly, forward motion is broken. Many of the fastest-accelerating players maintain a strongly inclined body angle for longer than those skaters who start less explosively.

Points to Remember

- It takes several running strides to accelerate.
- Use powerful, sprinting leg motions and push to full extension on every stride. Remember that all sprinting strides must have the same tempo (leg rhythm).
- Recover each returning leg completely. The skates and legs must return and pass each other in the V-diamond position.
- Each rapid running stride should take you farther than the preceding one. On the first step you are limited in the distance you can travel because your body is not yet in motion (you are overcoming inertia).
- Keep body weight inclined well forward.

- Leap *outward*—do not jump upward! Height off the ice should be minimal.
- The function of the edges is to form a solid wedge in the ice against which you vault yourself forward.
- Drive arms in a forward-backward motion, in rhythm and on the same line of force with your legs.
- Keep the hockey stick on the ice in a position that allows you to keep the puck well ahead of you as you accelerate. If you allow the puck to jam your body, you won't have enough room to skate.
- An explosive start is actually a process of falling. After much practice you will learn to control the fall, but while learning you may fall many times. For balance and stability, hold shoulders back, chest upright. Look straight ahead and keep your head and chin up.
- The cuts that the edges make in the ice should be short, well turned out, and deep. These indicate that force has been successfully concentrated over a very short distance (no longer than the length of the blade), allowing for explosive motion. Long marks in the ice indicate gliding strides rather than running strides. Gliding dissipates force and is a process of deceleration. Figure 7.3 diagrams the initial strides of an explosive front start.

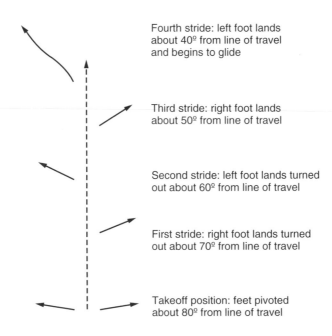

Fourth stride: left foot lands about 40º from line of travel and begins to glide

Third stride: right foot lands about 50º from line of travel

Second stride: left foot lands turned out about 60º from line of travel

First stride: right foot lands turned out about 70º from line of travel

Takeoff position: feet pivoted about 80º from line of travel

Figure 7.3   Front (forward) start, showing cuts in ice.

Figure 7.4, a-c shows incorrect marks traced in the ice during the front start. Note them and understand the mistakes that may cause them. Practice starts on clean ice so you can study your marks.

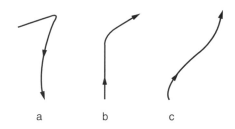

a   b   c

Figure 7.4 Marks on ice indicate different errors on initial strides of front (forward) start: *(a)* toe turned straight down; *(b)* blade contacted ice facing straight forward; *(c)* heel of blade contacted ice.

The marks shown in figure 7.4a indicate a short, well-turned cut. However, at some point during the push, the pushing toe turned to point straight down, causing the skate and leg to slip back on the flat of the blade. Result: no push, plus loss of balance.

The marks shown in figure 7.4b indicate that the skate blade made contact with the ice facing straight ahead instead of outward. This caused a glide. In order to push, it was first necessary to pivot the skate outward. Result: loss of quickness.

The marks shown in figure 7.4c indicate that the heel of the blade made contact with the ice. This caused the skate to glide. Result: slower leg speed.

Gliding may result from a variety of errors, including:

Inadequate inside edge on the contact skate

Weight too far back (on the heel) of the blade

Heel of the blade contacts the ice, forcing a glide

Insufficient knee bend

Body weight not inclined far enough forward

Insufficient turnout of contact skate (skate faces forward on touchdown rather than outward)

Slow or incomplete leg recovery

Side or Crossover Start

The side (crossover) start is an effective method of starting following a hockey stop. It can be used either to launch off in the opposite direction or to continue in the same direction. When a hockey stop is completed, the player is already turned sideways and positioned to start out explosively using the side start (figure 7.5).

The side start is a crossover move in which the outside leg pushes first (stride push against

Figure 7.5 Side (crossover) start, right over left.

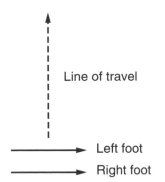

Line of travel

————————➤ Left foot

————————➤ Right foot

Figure 7.6 Side (crossover) start: feet perpendicular to the line of travel.

the inside edge) and the inside leg pushes second (X push against the outside edge). The inside leg drives under the body as the outside (trailing) skate crosses over in front of the inside skate and lands on its inside edge. As in the front start, the body weight must be projected low and outward (now to the side).

To perform an explosive side start, shift your weight as if you were pushing a heavy weight with your shoulder. As in the front start, the initial steps should be taken as rapid, powerful running steps. The combination of quickness (rapid leg speed), powerful leg drive, and distance covered yields an explosive start.

The side start is done as if you were leaping sideways along a line, crossing over as you move, and keeping your skates and body sideways to the intended line of travel (figure 7.6). This is critical—if one or both skates turn forward to face the line of travel, they will not grip the ice. The skates will glide forward and it will be impossible to do a crossover start.

The following instructions describe a start to the left (right-over-left crossover). To start to the right, reverse the instructions.

The First Stride

1. The left skate is the inside (leading) skate. Your skates must be perpendicular (sideways) to the intended line of travel and shoulder-width apart; keep your knees well bent (figure 7.7a). Place your weight over the inside edge of the *outside* (right) skate.

Stride Push

2. Push with the outside (right) leg. During the push, shift your weight sideways over the left outside edge, driving your body weight to the left (figure 7.7b).

X Push

3. Leap out to the side (left) while doing a right-over-left crossover. Thrust the inside (left) leg against its outside edge as the outside (right) skate begins to cross

a

Figure 7.7 Side (crossover) start sequence. *(continued)*

b

c

d

e

f

g

Figure 7.7 *(continued)*

over in front of the inside (left) skate. Drive it under your body to full extension (figure 7.7, c-d).

4. The right skate should land on the front two to three inches of its inside edge, turned approximately 70 to 75 degrees from the line of travel, with your body weight concentrated over the inside edge (figure 7.7e). The heel of the blade should not touch the ice.

Drive your body weight and crossing (right) knee as far out to the left as possible. Jumping up breaks the outward motion. Strive for distance, not height.

5. After thrusting, the left skate and leg (now the free skate and leg) must immediately return, pass the contact (right) skate (in the V-diamond position), and reach forward in preparation for becoming the new contact skate (figure 7.7f).

The Second Stride

1. As the right skate contacts the ice, it immediately becomes the new pushing skate.
2. One crossover is sufficient. Just prior to pushing with the right leg, pivot your hips to face forward (figure 7.7f). The next and all subsequent strides will be the powerful sprinting steps of the front start.
3. When the left skate takes the ice as the new contact skate, it should land on the toe (front two to three inches of inside edge), your body weight concentrated over the edge, heel off the ice (figure 7.7g), just as in the second step of the front start.
4. After thrusting, the right skate and leg (now the free skate and leg) must immediately return, pass the left skate (skates and legs in the V-diamond position), and reach forward to become the new contact skate.

Subsequent Strides

On the third or fourth stride the skates should begin to glide, and the angle of your upper body to the ice should gradually become more upright until, after five or six strides it reaches the forward stride position (approximately 45 degrees to the ice).

Points to Remember

- On the crossover the contact skate must touch down sideways (approximately 70 to 75 degrees from the line of travel) or the edge won't dig in properly. Figure 7.8 diagrams the cuts made in the ice when the side start sequence is correctly performed.

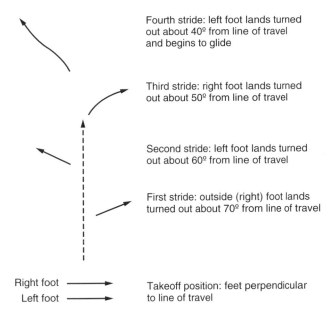

Fourth stride: left foot lands turned
out about 40º from line of travel
and begins to glide

Third stride: right foot lands turned
out about 50º from line of travel

Second stride: left foot lands turned
out about 60º from line of travel

First stride: outside (right) foot lands
turned out about 70º from line of travel

Right foot
Left foot

Takeoff position: feet perpendicular
to line of travel

Figure 7.8 Right-over-left side (crossover) start, showing cuts in ice.

- The outside leg push is used to shift body weight out to the side. The inside leg push is used to drive the body weight even further out to the side.
- The edges must grip the ice strongly.
- Drive each pushing leg directly against the grip. Do not let the pushing skate slip back.
- For balance and stability, hold shoulders back, chest upright. Look straight ahead and keep your head and chin up.

Backward Starts

It is important to start backward explosively from a stationary position so that you won't have to turn your back on the play. Defenders must be able to accelerate explosively and quickly to remain ahead of and always facing the opposition. Defenders who have not mastered backward starts must start forward and then wheel around backward to face the play. They are forced to turn their backs to the action, and risk being taken advantage of by a smart forward. This is one of the major no-nos in hockey.

When starting backward, you are limited in how much you can shift weight or angle the upper body backward in the direction of travel, because you would fall over backward. It is therefore not possible to accelerate as quickly when skating backward as when skating forward.

There are two methods of starting out backward. One is the straight backward start and the other is the backward crossover start. In games use the one that is more advantageous in the specific game situation. For example, a defender must not commit to a direction prematurely because the attacker might cut the other way. The advantage of the straight backward start is that the direction of travel is a straight line that keeps the defender straight ahead of, and feet neutral, to the attacker. If the attacker makes a move to one side, the defender is prepared to turn quickly to that side to cut off the attacker. However, the straight backward start is not quite as quick as the backward crossover start. If an attacker is pressing, the backward crossover start might be more advantageous.

The backward crossover start has a distinct disadvantage—it commits the defender to one side. This can create an opportunity for the attacker to break away in the opposite direction. A cagey forward will wait for the defender to cross over prematurely and use this opportunity to race the other way. When using a backward crossover start, be sure there is substantial space between the you and the opposition or you stand a good chance of "getting burned."

Note: In situations where the opposing forward is very closely pressing the defender, the defender might have to start forward, build speed, and then turn backward. But whenever possible, it is important to start backward facing the play.

The Straight Backward Start

As in all starts, the first few strides are critical. This start is used primarily in situations where the defender needs to keep his or her skates neutral to the opponent.

To perform the straight backward start, execute a sequence of backward C-cut pushes. The gliding skate must aim straight backward. The difference between the straight backward start and the straight backward stride is that the legs move much more rapidly on the initial steps of the start. The contact skate should glide as little as possible, but each pushing leg must still thrust and return through its full range of motion. See chapter 5 for details on the backward C-cut push procedure.

Note: Although the start requires a very rapid leg tempo, be sure to get full leg drive and full leg recovery.

1. Just as in the C-cut pushes of straight backward skating, the inside edge is employed as the thrusting edge. Pivot the heel of the thrusting skate outward, bend knees deeply, place weight over the pushing leg, and dig the inside edge into the ice in preparation for pushing (figure 7.9a).

2. Cut the C by thrusting against the inside edge. Use the front half of the blade length to push. The final thrust is made with the toe of the inside edge. Push powerfully and rapidly (figure 7.9b).

3. Push to full extension. The pushing leg must then recover rapidly so the other leg can immediately push (figure 7.9, c-e).

4. After several pushes you should approach top speed.

5. Swing your arms in rhythm and in the same line with your legs. The right arm goes back as the right leg thrusts forward and outward, and vice versa.

Points to Remember

- Explosive acceleration depends on powerful leg drive and rapid leg motion. Small, hopping steps, though rapid, provide little thrust—you end up going nowhere.

Note: You must cover distance quickly.

- Keep hips facing directly backward. If they turn sideways with each push, you will waddle from side to side rather than skate straight backward.
- Keep the contact (gliding) foot pointing straight backward.
- While executing the C-cut, be sure the entire blade length is in contact with the ice surface. If the heel lifts off the ice, you will be off balance.

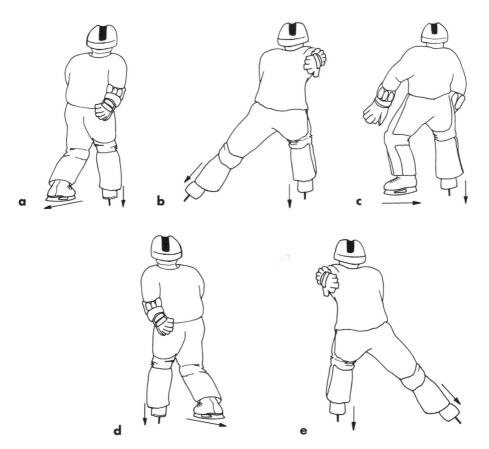

Figure 7.9 Straight backward start sequence.

• To avoid pitching forward over the curved toes, hold your shoulders back and your back upright. Look straight ahead and keep your head and chin up.

Backward Crossover Start

Many defenders feel they can start out faster with a backward crossover start than with the straight backward start. As with the straight backward start, the backward crossover start begins with the powerful C-cut thrust. Execute the C-cut thrust powerfully and quickly to full extension before crossing over (figure 7.10, a-b). Then drive the inside leg under your body (X push) as the outside leg (now the free leg) crosses over (figure 7.10, c-d). (See chapter 6, "Weaving Crossovers," for details of the procedure.) Figure 7.11 diagrams the backward crossover start.

Figure 7.10 Backward crossover start sequence.

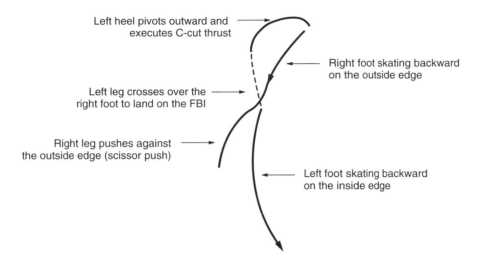

Left heel pivots outward and executes C-cut thrust

Right foot skating backward on the outside edge

Left leg crosses over the right foot to land on the FBI

Right leg pushes against the outside edge (scissor push)

Left foot skating backward on the inside edge

Figure 7.11   Pattern of backward crossover start.

Exercises for Improving Starts

These exercises are specifically designed to improve front, side, and backward starts.

Front Start Exercises

The following exercises help develop the coordination, edge control, and body angles necessary for explosive front starts.

Penguin Walk

To do this exercise, you walk across the ice on the "toes" in a penguin-like or duck-like manner.

1. Place your skates and knees in the exaggerated V-diamond position, heels together, toes apart, skates turned outward about 80 to 85 degrees from the line of travel.
2. Bend your knees deeply. Keep knees and toes well turned out.
3. Keeping your knees bent, roll in your ankles so that the lower leg and the inside edge of each skate form a strong angle with the ice; heels together, toes apart.

4. Place your weight over the front two to three inches of both inside edges and lift your heels so that only the fronts of the inside edges (toes) are in contact with the ice. Maintain the same edge angle and knee bend while standing in this position (figure 7.12a).

5. Now walk across the ice in this manner, always touching down on the front two to three inches of the engaged inside edge (45-degree angle), heel elevated, knee bent, knee and skate turned out, body weight pressing downward over the engaged edge (figure 7.12b).

6. To walk in this position, heels must face each other and toes must face outward (V-diamond position) as each skate passes the other.

7. The marks in the ice should be two to three inches long, indicating no glide.

Note: Do not let your heels touch the ice at any time during the penguin walk.

Penguin Run

a. Run in place on the toes (inside edges), maintaining the exaggerated penguin-like (V-diamond) position—heels facing in, knees and toes facing out. Keep heels off the ice with your weight on the front two to three inches of the inside edges as you run in place.

b. Now run between the blue lines. Do not allow the heel of the contact skate to touch the ice because this will force the skate to glide.

c. Now run between the blue lines and concentrate on pushing to full extension.

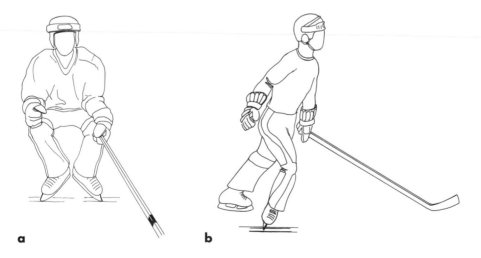

a   **b**

Figure 7.12 The penguin walk exercise.

Starts Against the Boards

This exercise trains you to . . .

- reach the knee of the contact skate forward for distance rather than upward for height,
- angle the upper body forward,
- fully extend the pushing leg while reaching the front knee forward, and
- maintain the turned-out (V-diamond) position of the skates and knees through the push and return.

To perform starts against boards:

Figure 7.13 Front starts at the boards.

1. Stand at arm's length from and facing the boards. Hold on to the boards with both hands.
2. Turn your skates and knees in the exaggerated V-diamond position, heels facing in, knees and toes facing out.
3. Angle your body forward but keep your back straight. Do not slouch.
4. Move the contact skate forward. It should pass the pushing skate in the V-diamond position. Keep heels facing in and toes facing out as each skate passes the other.
5. Now reach the knee of the contact skate forward until it just about touches the boards. The contact skate should touch down with your weight on the front two to three inches of the inside edge, turned outward about 80 to 85 degrees from the line of travel.
6. Simultaneously with reaching the knee of the contact skate forward (toward the boards), drive the pushing (back) leg to full extension (figure 7.13).
7. Alternate feet.
8. Repeat, now increasing the speed at which you can push and change feet.

Resistance Starts

This exercise helps to . . .

- teach you how to get and stay on the toes,
- train the contact skate to touch down on and push against the toes of the inside edges,

- feel the upper-body angle required for explosive starts, and
- push powerfully and to full extension.

Push another player across the ice while touching down only on the toes of the inside edges. The player moving backward should resist by doing a two-foot backward snowplow stop (see chapter 8, pages 138 and 139). Keep your skates and knees in the V-diamond position (heels together, toes apart) with heels off the ice (figure 7.14, a-b). Note the strong forward angle of the upper body of the pushing player in figure 7.14b.

a **b**

Figure 7.14 Resistance starts on toes.

Front Starts Over Hockey Sticks

Starts over hockey sticks help train the legs to drive harder and the upper body to shift out farther in order to achieve more distance on each starting step. Concentrate on driving your body weight outward for distance, not upward for height.

1. Team up with three other players of similar heights and abilities. Place four hockey sticks on the ice, as diagrammed in figure 7.15. The sticks should be spaced so that on the first three to four steps of the front start the players must shift their weight well forward and cover more distance on each progressive step of the start. Distances between the sticks should be arranged to accommodate each skater's size and ability. The distances should be challenging but not impossible to surmount. If the sticks are placed too close together, players merely jump upward to get over them rather than leap outward to get beyond them.

In the following "stick" exercises, the area between the first two sticks is the "no-zone." Do *not* step into this zone.

2. Face the hockey sticks and stand in the exaggerated V-diamond position with toes almost touching the first stick (figure 7.16a).

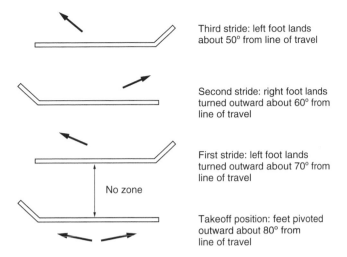

Third stride: left foot lands about 50° from line of travel

Second stride: right foot lands turned outward about 60° from line of travel

First stride: left foot lands turned outward about 70° from line of travel

No zone

Takeoff position: feet pivoted outward about 80° from line of travel

Figure 7.15 Front start over sticks; note angle of the skates to the line of travel.

3. Place your weight over the thrusting (right) skate, bend both knees, and dig the inside edge of the thrusting skate into the ice (45 degrees). Shift your body weight well forward (figure 7.16a).

4. Leap beyond the first two sticks (avoiding the no-zone) and land past the second stick on the toe (front two to three inches) of the left inside edge. Make certain the left skate lands facing outward (maintain the V-diamond position), body weight over it, heel off the ice (figure 7.16b). The cut in the ice should be short and facing outward, indicating that the skate did not glide.

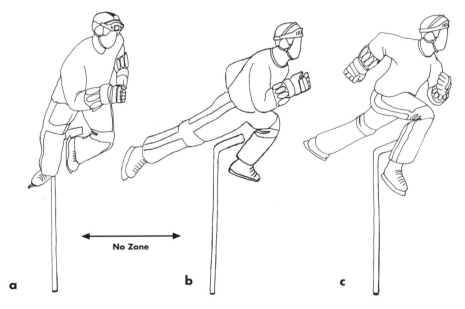

No Zone

a　　　　　b　　　　　c

Figure 7.16 Front start over sticks.

5. Repeat, now thrusting with the left leg and landing beyond the third stick on the toe (front two to three inches) of the right inside edge, body weight over it, with the right skate facing outward and heel off the ice (figure 7.16c). Again, the cut in the ice should be short and facing outward, indicating that the skate did not glide.

6. Thrust again with the right leg, landing past the fourth stick on the left inside edge, with the left skate facing outward and heel off the ice. After passing the fourth stick, sprint until you reach top speed. Your body angle should rise gradually until, at top speed, it is approximately 45 degrees to the ice.

7. As this exercise becomes easier, place the sticks farther apart. Force the legs to drive hard and your weight to shift farther out to clear the sticks, but don't make it impossible. Remember: Leap out to get beyond the sticks, not up to get over them.

8. Repeat, now using the left skate and leg to make the initial thrust. The legs must be equally capable of making the all-important first thrust.

9. Take the sticks away and see if you can go as far as or farther than you did with the sticks. Move your legs as rapidly as possible. Do not sacrifice leg speed in trying to go farther.

Sprint Starts

Start from the goal line. Take two or three running strides and then sprint to the first blue line. Remember: Combine quickness, power, and distance on the starting strides. Time yourself; try to improve your time. The more adept you become with these starts, the better your time should become.

Side Start Exercises

The following exercises help develop the coordination, edge control, and body weight projection necessary for explosive side starts. Practice them using both the left and right legs to perform the initial thrust.

Walking Crossovers

Stand facing perpendicular (sideways) to the intended direction of travel. Walk to the left, crossing the right skate over in front of the left skate as you walk sideways. The left (leading or inside) skate always steps onto its outside edge, then crosses under the body to push (X push). The right (trailing or outside) skate, after pushing (stride push), crosses over in front of the left skate and steps onto its inside edge. Start on one sideboard and walk all across the rink. It is imperative to keep your skates sideways to the line of travel as you walk.

Running Crossovers

Follow the procedure for walking crossovers, but now run sideways along the line of travel. Stay on the toes (front two to three inches of the edges) as you run. Keep heels off the ice throughout this exercise. Remember: Run outward, not upward.

Lateral Leaping Crossovers

Repeat the running crossovers, now leaping each crossover sequence. Try to get as much sideways distance as possible from each stride. Use the push from the outside leg to shift your weight out to the side. Use the push from the inside leg to shift your weight even farther out to the side. Push to full extension on all pushes and keep the heel of each contact skate off the ice.

Zigzag Leaping Crossovers

Start from the goal line and skate forward along the boards (figure 7.17). Stop at the near blue line. Do lateral leaping crossovers (left over right) along the blue line across to the opposite sideboards. Stop. Skate forward to the far blue line, stop, and do lateral leaping crossovers (right over left) along the blue line to the opposite sideboards. Stop, skate forward along the boards to the goal line, and stop again.

Note: Leap outward on all pushes. Stay on your toes and keep heels off the ice on the leaping crossovers. As always, strive for distance, not height, on all crossovers.

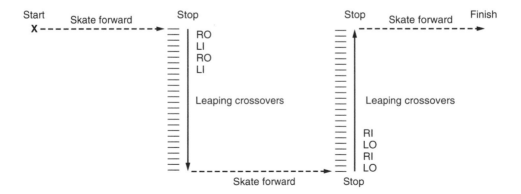

Figure 7.17 Leaping crossovers.

Leaping Crossovers on Whistle

On a whistle signal, rapidly move sideways to the left, using leaping crossovers (right over left). Get as much lateral distance and move your legs as quickly as possible. On a second signal, stop and leap out to the right (left over right). Alternate directions on each whistle signal. Keep heels off the ice during the leaping crossovers.

Note: Keep your skates and body facing sideways (at right angles) to the line of travel on all the side start exercises.

Side Starts Over Hockey Sticks

Crossover starts over hockey sticks train the legs to drive harder and the upper body to shift out farther to the side in order to achieve more distance on the first three to four steps of the crossover start. Concentrate on driving the body weight outward for distance, not upward for height.

The sticks should be spaced to challenge each player's ability. The idea is to train players to use their legs and body weight to project outward. In this exercise, each starting step should cover more distance than the previous one.

Team up with three other players of similar height and ability. Place four hockey sticks on the ice, following the guidelines given for front starts over hockey sticks (figure 7.18).

1. Stand with both skates parallel to the sticks (sideways to the intended direction of travel), to the right of the sticks. Place the left skate close to and still parallel to the first stick, (right skate parallel to the left), skates slightly

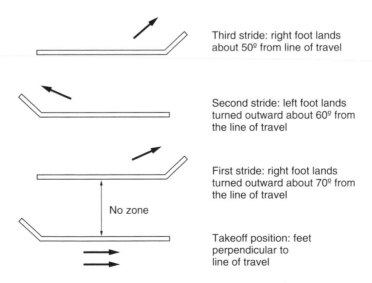

Third stride: right foot lands about 50º from line of travel

Second stride: left foot lands turned outward about 60º from the line of travel

First stride: right foot lands turned outward about 70º from the line of travel

No zone

Takeoff position: feet perpendicular to line of travel

Figure 7.18 Side (crossover) start over sticks; note position of feet to the line of travel.

wider than shoulder-width apart. Knees must be well bent, with body weight over the outside (trailing) skate.

2. Do a right-over-left crossover start. Thrust the right leg (stride push) to full extension. Use this push to shift your weight outward to the left (figure 7.19a).

3. Drive the left leg under your body (X push), and at the same time do a leaping crossover, crossing the right skate in front of the left. Land beyond the second stick (not in the "no-zone"), on the toe (front two to three inches) of the right inside edge with the right skate still sideways (70 to 75 degrees) to the line of travel (figure 7.19b).

Note: Be sure to keep the heel of the landing skate off the ice. If the heel touches the ice, you will glide.

4. While still on the toe of your right skate, pivot your hips, chest, and shoulders 90 degrees until you face fully forward in the front start position. Now thrust the right leg against the right inside edge as you would in a front start. Leap forward and land past the third stick on the toe (front two to three inches) of the left inside edge, with your weight over it and heel off the ice. The left skate should touch down facing outward (as in the front start), enabling the inside edge to immediately grip the ice.

5. Thrust again with the left leg and leap forward as in the front start. Leap beyond the fourth stick, landing on the right inside edge with the right skate facing outward. Continue sprinting until you reach full speed. Your

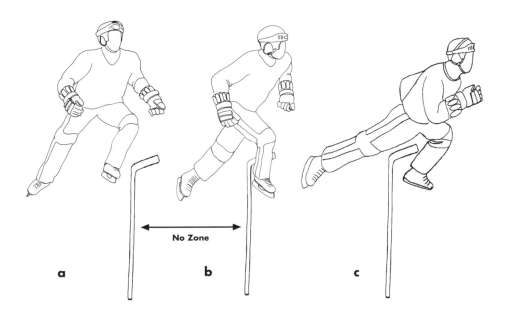

Figure 7.19 Side starts over sticks.

body angle should rise gradually until it reaches the skating angle of the forward stride (approximately 45 degrees).

6. Concentrate on leaping out beyond (farther than) the sticks rather than up over (higher than) them. Remember: distance, not height.

To execute the exercise in the opposite direction, face the other way. The right skate is now close to the first stick. Leap to the right, crossing left over right.

Take the sticks away and see if you can get more distance in the same time or less than before. Measure how far outward you travel on the first three strides of the start (one crossover, two forward steps) in as short a time as possible. Keep trying to increase the distance and shorten the time. Remember, that more distance covered in the same or less time equates with a faster start!

Side Starts Over the Goal Crease

The purpose of this exercise is to train the legs to push and the body weight to shift far out to the side. More weight projection helps achieve greater distance on the starting strides. It is similar to side starts over sticks; the outer line of the goal crease is the target that the first contact skate must reach.

Note: This exercise is best used for older, more elite-level skaters. Young skaters cannot achieve (nor is it advantageous for them to achieve) this distance.

1. Stand with feet parallel to the goal line (sideways to the line of travel), prepared to skate to the first blue line. Place the left (leading or inside) skate on the goal line, right skate parallel to the left, skates slightly wider than shoulder-width apart, knees bent, body weight over the outside (right) skate.
2. Do a leaping crossover, right over left, and land on or close to the outer crease line. Land on the toe (front two to three inches) of the right inside edge, with the right skate almost parallel to the outer line of the crease (about 70 to 75 degrees from the line of travel). Now pivot forward and sprint to the blue line.
3. Repeat with a left-over-right crossover start.

Sprint Starts

Start from the goal line. Using the side (crossover) start, take two or three running steps and then sprint to the blue line. Stop. Start again and sprint to the far blue line. Stop. Start again and sprint to the goal line at the far end of the rink. Stop. Alternate the side to which you start and try to better the starts in both directions.

Stops and Starts

Practice stops and starts, alternating direction of the stops and starts. Time yourself. Try to improve your starting times in both directions. (See chapter 8 for a detailed description of hockey stops.)

Backward Start Exercises

Straight Backward Start

Stand close to and facing the boards. With your weight over the left (pushing) leg, bend the left knee deeply and dig the left inside edge into the ice. Aim the right (gliding) skate straight back. Do a backward C-cut push with the left inside edge, using powerful, rapid leg drive to execute the thrust. Bring the thrusting skate back under your body as rapidly as possible after completing the push. Now execute a backward C-cut thrust with the right leg. Cut a total of three C-cut thrusts, moving your legs as rapidly as possible. Be sure to travel straight back. Come to a stop after the third C-cut and check to see how far you have traveled after three pushes. Repeat, trying to increase the distance and shorten the time. Repeat the drill, now using the right leg to perform the initial push.

Straight Backward Start With Resistance

Working against resistance forces players to push correctly and more powerfully on straight backward starts.

Perform the previous exercise now pulling a player who resists by doing a forward snowplow stop as you do a straight backward start. The resisting player should hold one end of a hockey stick as you hold the other end. Keep the stick at chest height and horizontal to the ice. Refer to "Resistance Exercise," chapter 5, for the procedure.

Backward Sprint Starts

Start from the goal line and time yourself to the first blue line as you do backward C-cuts. As you practice try to increase your distances and lower your times. Alternate the starting leg each time. Each leg must develop the power and coordination required for making the initial thrust. With lots of practice you should be able to significantly improve your times.

Backward Crossover Start Exercises

Backward Crossover Starts

Perform the straight backward start exercise (page 129), but do it using a series of backward crossovers. The first push (C-cut) is done with the outside leg. Push the C-cut to full extension before crossing it over. Drive the inside leg under your body (X push) as the outside leg crosses over in front of the inside skate. Remember: A third (neutralizing) step onto the inside edge is necessary before continuing to skate backward. A third push is also necessary; it is another C-cut thrust and is done with the same leg as did the first C-cut push. Concentrate on maximizing all three pushes. Alternate right-over-left with left-over-right crossover starts. (See chapter 6, "Weaving Crossovers," pages 100-104, for details of the procedure.) As in all starts, it is imperative to execute all pushes powerfully and rapidly.

Backward Crossover Resistance Starts

Working against resistance forces players to push correctly and with more power on backward crossover starts. Perform the previous exercise, but now pulling a player who creates resistance by doing a forward snowplow stop as you do the backward crossover start. The resisting player should hold one end of a hockey stick as you hold the other end. Keep the stick at chest height and horizontal to the ice.

Backward Crossover Sprint Starts

Using the backward crossover start, time yourself from the goal line to the first blue line. Repeat; now time yourself from the goal line to the center red line. Now time yourself from the goal line to the far blue line. Use only one or two backward crossovers to start out; skate straight backward the rest of the way. Be sure to alternate the initial pushing leg of the backward crossover start.

Forward Versus Defender

Practice starts with another skater, one acting as forward, the other as defender. See chapter 5, page 76, for a description of this exercise.

chapter 8

Stops for Being Able to Halt on a Dime

Coaches spend much time teaching their players to "stop on a dime." Stops are an essential part of the game, as vital as explosive starts. Mastering all the stops will enable you to use the stop most appropriate for the situation at hand. In games you sometimes need to jam on the brakes. At other times you have to stop and change direction instantaneously. And there are times when it is best to slow down or stop gradually.

Forward Stops

The forward stops covered in this chapter progress from the most basic to the most difficult.

Forward Two-Foot Snowplow Stop

The two-foot snowplow stop—like the skier's snowplow—is the easiest stop to learn and therefore the first stop taught to beginning skaters. In game situations it is used mainly for slowing down or stopping very gradually. It is inadequate for very sudden stops.

Figure 8.1 Two-foot snowplow stop.

1. Glide straight ahead on two skates, feet shoulder-width apart.

2. Turn both heels outward so that your toes face each other in an inverted V (pigeon-toed) position. Keep your body facing the direction of travel.

3. Using *slight* inside edges on both skates, scrape against the ice. As you scrape against the ice, bend your knees and force your heels still farther apart (figure 8.1). Try to bring up "snow" with the inside edges.

Points to Remember

- Keep your body weight on the balls of your feet as you scrape the ice. If you try to scrape the ice with your heels, the inside edges may catch the ice, and stopping will be difficult.
- Keep shoulders back, back straight, eyes and head up. If you lean forward, you will pitch over the curved toes.
- Use slight inside edges to stop. If you edge too deeply, the edges will dig into the ice rather than scrape the ice, making a stop almost impossible.
- Try to bring up snow as you scrape the ice; don't try to cut into it.
- Keep the entire blade lengths of both skates in contact with the ice. Lifting the heels will cause you to pitch over the curved toes.

Forward One-Foot Snowplow Stop

The forward one-foot snowplow stop is sometimes used in game situations. Defenders may use it, for instance, when they are skating forward but want to decelerate to prepare for skating backward, or if they want to stop very gradually. Goalies frequently use a one-foot snowplow stop.

Figure 8.2 One-foot snowplow stop.

1. Glide straight forward on the flat of the left skate. Keep the left skate centered under your body weight.
2. Holding the right skate somewhat out in front, turn that toe inward (pigeon-toed) and press the right skate against the ice, using a slight inside edge to scrape against the ice.
3. Bend your right knee to concentrate your weight downward over the right skate and scrape the ice with the right inside edge, skate still in the pigeon-toed position (figure 8.2).
4. Scrape the ice with the ball of the foot, not the heel.
5. Except for pigeon-toeing and scraping against the ice with only one skate rather than two, the stop is performed in the same way as the two-foot snowplow.
6. Repeat, using the left skate to pigeon-toe and execute the stop. The right skate will now glide straight ahead.

Figure 8.3 Correct position for T-stop.

Figure 8.4 Incorrect position for T-stop.

Figure 8.5 T-stop on one foot.

T-Stop

The T-stop is often used when players come to the bench or to the face-off circle. It is rarely used in situations when sudden, well-balanced stops are called for.

1. Glide straight forward on the flat of the right skate.

2. Lift the left skate and place it behind the right skate, turning the toe outward so that the turned skate is perpendicular to the gliding (front) skate. Your feet should form an inverted T.

3. Place the outside edge of the back (left) skate on the ice in this perpendicular position. Apply pressure to the outside edge and bend the left knee. Apply gradual but constant pressure to the ice with the outside edge. Use the ball of your foot, not the heel, to press against (scrape) the ice (figure 8.3).

4. Keep your shoulders level as you lean back. If you lower the back (trailing) shoulder excessively, you will lose your balance and could fall backward.

5. Scrape the ice with the outside edge. If you lean forward you will be forced to drag the inside edge (figure 8.4) and won't be able to stop efficiently.

6. Shoulders, chest, and hips should face forward (the direction of travel) while executing the T-stop.

7. Advanced skaters often do a T-stop on just the back skate; the front skate is actually off the ice (figure 8.5).

Be sure to master both the one-foot snowplow and the T-stop—together they are the components of the hockey stop.

Hockey Stop

Hockey demands that players instantly stop to stay with the play or change directions as the action shifts. The hockey stop is the quickest and most sudden of all stops and is therefore the one used when skating fast. Not only does this stop allow players to stop suddenly. When properly executed it is also a very stable stop. Players must be able to stop immediately while always facing the action.

The hockey stop involves turning sideways (90 degrees) to the direction of travel.

1. Skate straight forward. Glide very briefly in preparation for stopping. Now turn your shoulders, chest, hips, knees, and feet sharply to the left (figure 8.6a). If this maneuver were done on a straight line it would be a 90-degree change of direction (figure 8.6b).

2. To stop, first unbend your knees slightly to release your weight. Do this as you begin to turn sideways. Then bend your knees deeply and apply your weight firmly downward toward the ice. This downward pressure combined with having turned sideways causes the edges to

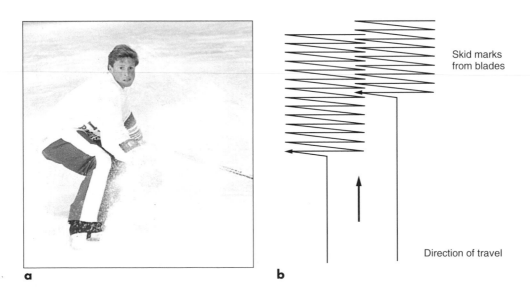

Skid marks
from blades

Direction of travel

a   b

Figure 8.6 Hockey stop to the left: (a) deep knee bend; (b) diagram showing 90-degree change of direction.

scrape the ice, allowing you to stop. The greater the knee bend and downward pressure, the quicker you will stop.

3. The hockey stop is generally executed with the body weight distributed approximately 60 percent on the front (outside) skate and 40 percent on the back (inside) skate. This guideline may vary with game conditions.

4. The front (outside) skate scrapes the ice with its inside edge, while the back (inside) skate scrapes the ice with its outside edge. A sudden stop causes snow to fly. The faster you are going and the more suddenly you press your weight downward toward the ice as you stop, the more snow you will scrape.

5. Scrape the ice with the balls of the feet. Scraping with the heels causes the edges to dig into the ice and makes stopping difficult.

6. To stop to the right, mirror the procedures just described.

7. During the stop, the upper body usually turns sideways along with the hips, knees, and feet. This puts you in an excellent position to use a side (crossover) start, either to skate forward in the same direction or in the opposite direction.

When you need to stop and then start out skating backward in the direction from which you just came, the following variation of the hockey stop is sometimes used: During the stop, keep your chest and shoulders facing forward. Do not turn them fully sideways as you turn your hips, knees, and feet (figure 8.7). Your upper body is now prepared to start backward quickly and explosively using a backward crossover start (see chapter 7).

Figure 8.7 Hockey stop: upper body faces forward.

Points to Remember

- As you stop the skates should be shoulder-width or even slightly wider apart. If they are too close together, balance is precarious. You will also be in a poor position to shift your weight sideways into the upcoming start.

- Keep your back straight, shoulders level to the ice, eyes and head up. The back (trailing) shoulder corresponds to the inside shoulder on a curve; lowering it may cause you to lose your balance.

- Keep the entire blade lengths of both skates on the ice during the stop. Lifting the heels will cause you to pitch forward over the toes of your skates.

- It is essential to glide briefly before turning sideways to stop. This allows for the release of weight in preparation for stopping. If you don't release your weight, turning sideways will be almost impossible.

One-Foot Stops

One-foot stops are similar in execution to the hockey stop, except that the body weight is concentrated on only one skate. There are two variations— the *front-foot stop* and the *back-foot stop.*

1. Front-foot: Skate straight forward, gliding on the right skate, and pick up the left skate. Turn your body 90 degrees to the left. Bend your right knee and scrape the ice with the inside edge of the right (front) skate until you stop. Keep the left (back) skate off the ice during the stop (figure 8.8). Be sure to scrape the ice with the ball of the foot, not with the heel. Repeat on the left skate, turning your body and stopping to the right.

2. Back-foot: Skate straight forward, gliding on the right skate, left skate off the ice. Turn your body 90 degrees to the right, bend your right knee, and scrape the ice with the outside edge of the right (back) skate. Keep the left (front) skate off the ice during the stop. Be sure to scrape the ice with the ball of the foot, not with the heel. When using the left skate as the back foot, turn sideways to the left.

Figure 8.8 Front-foot stop.

To stop with the outside edge of the back skate, you must lean much farther back than in the front-foot or hockey stops, but otherwise the stop is executed similarly. If you lower the back (trailing) shoulder, the skate may slip out from under you, causing you to fall backward.

Backward Stops

Backward stops are imperative for playing defense or for coming to a halt when skating backward.

Backward Two-Foot Snowplow Stop

This stop is used to stop quickly and efficiently when skating backward.

1. Glide straight backward on two skates, keeping them about shoulder-width apart. Rotate the toes of both skates outward while rotating the heels inward. Your feet should approximate a wide-based V position.

2. Push the toes of both skates farther apart. As you do this the heels will also separate to about shoulder-width apart.

3. As the toes rotate outward, press against the ice with *slight* inside edges of both skates and scrape the ice with the edges.

4. Bend your knees deeply as the edges scrape the ice. The more your knees bend, the more pressure you will exert downward against the ice and the quicker you'll stop.

5. *Scrape the ice equally with both skates* by keeping your weight equally distributed. Use the balls of the feet, not the heels, to scrape the ice (figure 8.9).

Figure 8.9 Two-foot backward snowplow stop.

A well-executed backward snowplow stop leaves the player in a good position to start forward. To thrust off forward, shift all your weight onto the leg that is going to push, dig the inside edge of the thrusting skate into the ice, bend the knee more deeply, and push off (figure 8.10).

Note: It is important to stop with the heels no wider than shoulder-width apart. If the heels separate much farther than this, there will be a delay in getting the thrusting leg re-centered under the body for a forward thrust.

Figure 8.10 Stop backward, start forward.

Backward One-Foot Snowplow Stop

The backward one-foot snowplow stop is similar to the backward two-foot snowplow stop except that only one foot executes the stop.

1. Glide straight backward on the flats of both skates.

2. To stop with the right skate, shift your weight over the right skate and rotate the toe of the right skate outward (the heel rotates inward).

Figure 8.11 One-foot backward stop.

3. Bend your right knee deeply and scrape the ice with the inside edge of the right skate, using a slight inside edge. Scrape the ice with the ball of the foot (figure 8.11).

This stop leaves you in excellent position for an explosive front start, because the stopping skate is centered under your body weight and turned outward in the front start position. All you have to do is dig the inside edge deeper into the ice, bend your knee more deeply, and thrust off forward.

Points to Remember

- Lean slightly forward, away from the stop, but keep your back straight and head up.
- Keep hips, chest, and shoulders facing straight ahead.
- It is not possible to execute this stop if the skates are parallel to each other.

Exercises for Improving Stops

The following exercises are designed to develop the coordination, edge control, and body weight distribution needed to execute effective stops.

Forward Snowplow Stops

The following exercises can be practiced both for two-foot and one-foot snowplow stops.

Stand and Scrape

Stand in place and scrape the ice simultaneously with both skates by pressing the skates apart in a pigeon-toed position. Try to bring up snow by using the balls of the feet and slight inside edges to scrape the ice.

O Drill

These develop the turn-out/turn-in coordination necessary for snowplow stops. For a detailed description of the exercise, see chapter 2, pages 21-22.

Two-Foot Snowplow

Start at the sideboards and skate forward across the ice, arms extended and holding the hockey stick horizontally at chest height. This will prevent you from leaning on it when stopping. Stop at the other side with a two-foot snowplow stop. Do not touch the boards.

One-Foot Snowplow

Repeat, using the one-foot snowplow stop. Alternate using the left and right skates as the snowplowing skate.

One-Foot Snowplow Stops and Starts

Start from the goal line and skate forward, stopping and then starting again as you reach the first blue line, the center red line, the second blue line, and the far goal line. Use one-foot snowplow stops at each line, alternating left and right skates as the stopping skate.

Backward Snowplow Stops

Backward snowplow stops can be practiced in the same way as the forward snowplow exercises just described. Remember that the direction of travel and skate turnout are reversed.

Team-Up Hockey Stop

If you are just learning the hockey stop you'll find it helpful to work with an instructor or partner. This allows you to concentrate on learning to coordinate the skates, knees, and hips without having to worry about controlling the upper body. The upper body will be controlled by the instructor or partner.

1. Face the instructor (or partner), holding a hockey stick horizontally at chest height between you. The instructor will skate backward while you glide forward on both skates.
2. On the instructor's signal, turn your hips and feet 90 degrees to the right and bend your knees. Keeping your skates parallel to each other, stop by scraping the ice with the inside edge of the front skate and the outside edge of the back skate (figure 8.12).

Figure 8.12 Team-up hockey stop.

Repeat, turning your hips, knees, and skates to the left. Be sure to practice on the direction that is more difficult.

Hockey Stops on the Whistle

1. Stand at the goal line, prepared to skate forward.
2. On a whistle signal, skate forward.
3. On the next whistle briefly glide, then do a hockey stop facing the sideboards to your left. Be sure to come to a complete stop.
4. On the next whistle skate forward again in the same direction.
5. On the next whistle stop again, facing the same way.

Do this the entire length of the ice. Coming back, stop, facing the same sideboards (now to your right). This way you will work on hockey stops to both sides.

Exercises for Improving Stops and Starts

When hockey players come to sudden stops, they do so knowing they might have to immediately start out again suddenly and explosively. Stops, in fact, set up the upcoming starts, so the quality of a stop affects the quality of the upcoming start. For example, stopping with skates too close together limits your ability to shift your weight in the desired direction to start, thereby limiting the distance you can achieve on the first starting stride. Stopping on unbent knees leaves you uncoiled and unable to push into the next start. You are flat-footed and out of the play. Since stops and starts are interrelated, they should be practiced together as well as separately. The following exercises combine them.

When practicing stops and starts it is important to stop equally to both sides and to alternate the initial thrusting leg of the start. To do this skate up one length of the ice, always stopping to face the same sideboards (i.e., to your left). Skating back down the ice, stop facing the same sideboards (i.e., now to your right). While skating up the ice you will always stop facing to the left and use left-over-right crossovers to restart. While coming back you will stop facing to the right and use right-over-left crossover starts. Remember to give the weaker side extra attention.

Hockey Stops With Front and Side Starts

Exercise 1

1. Start from the goal line using a front (forward) start and sprint to the first blue line. Stop quickly by doing a hockey stop to the left (figure 8.13a).
2. Start out explosively using a side (left-over-right crossover) start, and skate forward in the same direction (figure 8.13, b-c). Do one crossover, then pivot forward and sprint to the center red line. Stop to the left as before.
3. Do another crossover start (left-over-right) and sprint forward to the second blue line. Stop to the left as before.

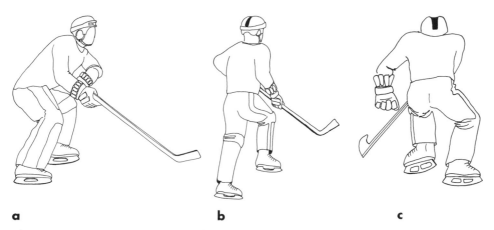

a   **b**   **c**

Figure 8.13   Exercise 1: Stop and start, continuing in same direction.

4. Do another left-over-right crossover start and sprint forward to the far goal line. Stop to the left.
5. Repeat the exercise, skating back down the ice, stopping and starting to the other side (facing the same sideboards which are now to your right).

Variation

Repeat the exercise but instead of stopping and starting at the lines, stop and start on whistle signals.

Exercise 2

In this exercise all stops and starts again face the same sideboards.

1. Start explosively from the goal line with a front start and sprint to the first blue line. Stop quickly with a hockey stop to the left (facing the sideboards on your left; figure 8.14a).

2. Start again with a right-over-left crossover start (figure 8.14, b-c) and sprint forward in the opposite direction (to the original goal line). Stop to the right, facing the same sideboards.

3. Reverse directions again by using a left-over-right crossover start. This time sprint forward to the center red line. Stop to the left.

4. Repeat step 2 (return to original goal line).

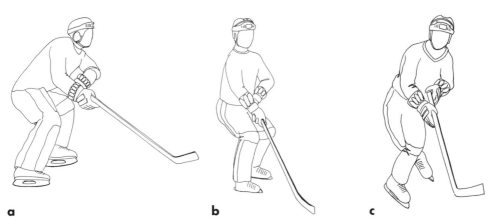

a   **b**   **c**

Figure 8.14 Exercise 2: Stop and start, continuing in opposite direction.

5. Reverse directions, using a left-over-right crossover start, and sprint forward to the far blue line. Stop to the left.

6. Repeat step 2 again (return to original goal line).

7. Reverse once more, using a left-over-right crossover start. Sprint forward to the far goal line and stop to the left.

8. Repeat step 2 (return to original goal line).

9. Repeat the exercise, stopping and starting to the other sides.

Variation

Repeat the exercise, but instead of stopping and starting at the lines, stop and start on whistle signals.

The stops in the following exercises are described for stopping to the left.

Exercise 3

Do a hockey stop to your left, body weight primarily on the front (outside) skate.

1. To continue in the same direction: After stopping, shift your weight far out to the right; it had been over the right inside edge, and now it is over the right outside edge. You are ready for a left-over-right crossover start. The stride push is the first push, and the X push is the second.

2. To skate back in the opposite direction: Keep your weight over the right inside edge. You have two options:

   a. Pivot your hips to face forward and do a front start.

   b. Do a right-over-left crossover start; as you push with the right leg, shift your weight far out to the left until it is over the left outside edge. Now drive into the crossover start using both the stride push and the X push.

Stops are usually performed with about 60 percent of the body weight over the front (outside) foot. However, there are exceptions to this, as explained in the following exercise.

Exercise 4

Perform a hockey stop to the left, with your body weight primarily over the back (inside) foot.

1. To continue in the same direction, you may choose to do either a front start or a side start.

   a. To use a front start, shift your weight from the left outside edge onto the left inside edge. Now quickly pivot your hips to face fully forward, and do a front start.

   b. To use a side start, shift your weight from the left outside edge onto the left inside edge. Continue shifting your weight far out to the right until it is over the right outside edge. Now execute a left-over-right crossover start (figure 8.14, b and c).

2. To skate back in the opposite direction, start with a right-over-left crossover start. Just shift your weight farther out over the left outside edge and execute the side start (figure 8.13, b and c).

Note: A front start in the opposite direction is possible, but a back-foot stop leaves you much better prepared to do a crossover start. The front start requires that you pivot your hips and chest to face forward before pushing. This takes valuable time that may slow down the starting process.

Figure 8.15 Start backward, using backward crossover start.

Forward Stops/Backward Starts

Assume this game scenario. You have been skating forward but the play dictates that you stop. Upon stopping you realize you must now quickly start out backward. In this situation, choose a forward stop that will prepare you to start backward quickly. You have two choices:

1. A one-foot snowplow stop.

2. A hockey stop with your weight primarily over the front (outside) foot.

It may be advantageous to use the hockey stop variation in which your upper body does not turn fully sideways as you stop (see figure 8.7, page 137). If using the one-foot snowplow stop, the stopping foot of the snowplow (which corresponds to the front foot of the hockey stop) becomes the initial thrusting leg of the backward start. Similarly, the front foot of the hockey stop becomes the initial thrusting leg of the backward start. The initial push of every backward start is the C-cut.

Because the front leg of the forward stop will become the thrusting leg of the backward start, it is critical to keep your weight primarily over the front skate while stopping. Your body weight is then correctly positioned over the pushing (C-cut) leg to drive into the backward push (figure 8.15a). Too many players stop with their weight almost completely over the back skate, and as a result cannot push effectively into the backward start.

When doing a backward crossover start, be sure to use the X push as well as the C-cut push (figure 8.15, b-d).

Note: When starting out backward from any hockey stop position, the hips must turn 90 degrees (one-quarter turn) during the start to face the new line of travel (backward). Turn your hips during the C-cut thrust. Do not turn them before the C-cut as this will delay your start. Do not turn them farther than one-quarter turn or the new line of travel will be altered; you will travel an S-pattern rather than straight backward.

Exercise 1

Use this exercise to improve the combination of forward stops with straight backward starts.

1. Glide straight forward on the right skate with the left skate off the ice. Stop (turning to the left) on the right skate. This is a front-foot hockey stop.
2. Keeping the left skate off the ice, roll the right skate onto its inside edge and bend the right knee so the edge and the lower leg form a strong (approximately 45-degree) angle to the ice. Execute a backward C-cut push with your right leg.
3. During the push, shift your weight onto the flat of the left skate and glide straight backward on the left skate.
4. Stop.

Mirror the procedure and repeat the drill, stopping on and executing the backward C-cut push with the left leg.

Exercise 2

Perform this exercise to improve the combination of forward stops with backward crossover starts.

1. Perform the previous exercise. However, as you execute the backward C-cut thrust with the right leg, shift your weight onto and skate backward on the outside edge of your left skate rather than the flat of the blade.
2. Use the left outside edge to execute the X push. Cross the right skate over to take the ice gliding backward on its inside edge as the pushing leg drives under the body.
3. Stop.

Mirror the procedure, executing the C-cut thrust with the left leg and the X push with the right leg.

Exercise 3

1. Do a front start at one sideboards and sprint forward across the ice. Execute the initial push of the start with your right leg.

2. Stop, using a hockey stop to the left, at the opposite sideboards and prepare to start out backward.

3. Do a right-over-left backward crossover start and sprint backward to your original position.

4. Stop at the original sideboards using a one-foot backward snowplow stop with the right skate, and prepare to start skating forward again.

5. Do a front start and sprint forward across the ice. Execute the initial push of the start with your left leg.

6. Stop at the opposite sideboards, now stopping to the right, and prepare to skate backward.

7. Do a left-over-right backward crossover start and sprint backward to your original position.

8. Stop at the original sideboards using a one-foot backward snowplow stop with the left skate, and prepare to skate forward again.

9. Keep repeating the exercise. Each time you stop, alternate the stopping side and the stopping leg. This also means that you must alternate the leg that performs the initial thrust of the subsequent forward or backward start.

10. Repeat the exercise. Each time you begin skating backward now do a straight backward start and skate backward using the straight backward stride.

11. Repeat the exercise. Now use weaving (alternating) backward crossovers to skate backward.

Variation

Repeat the exercise, now skating the length of the ice and using whistle signals to command the stops and starts.

Exercise 4

The following exercise is diagrammed in figure 8.16. The pattern diagrammed can be used for a variety of drills.

1. Start from one corner of the rink with a front start. Sprint forward diagonally across the ice to the blue line at the opposite sideboards; stop.

2. Execute a straight backward start and sprint backward along the blue line across the ice; stop.

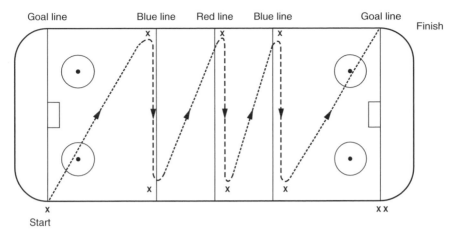

Figure 8.16 Stops and starts, alternating forward and backward skating.

3. Execute a front start and sprint forward diagonally across the ice to the center red line at the opposite sideboards; stop.

4. Execute a straight backward start and sprint backward along the red line across the ice; stop.

5. Execute a front start and sprint forward diagonally across the ice to the blue line at the opposite sideboards; stop.

6. Execute a straight backward start and sprint backward along the blue line across the ice; stop.

7. Execute a front start and sprint forward diagonally across the ice to the opposite corner; stop.

8. Repeat the exercise, starting from that corner. Stop to the other side and use the other leg to execute the initial thrust of each start.

Note: Alternate straight backward striding with weaving (alternating) backward crossovers to sprint backward.

Variations

Try these variations:

1. Repeat the previous exercise, now using backward crossover starts.

2. Repeat the exercise, now skating forward all the time. Use hockey stops and crossover starts throughout.

Exercise 5

1. Repeat the previous exercise as follows: Start out from one corner skating backward. Use a straight backward start. Sprint backward diagonally across the ice to the first blue line at the opposite sideboards. Stop, using a one-foot backward snowplow stop.

2. Do a front start, using the stopping leg of the backward stop as the initial pushing leg of the front start. Sprint forward along the blue line back across the ice; stop.

3. Continue in this manner until you reach the finishing corner as described in the previous exercise.

Variation

Repeat the exercise, but start backward, always using backward crossover starts.

Note: It is imperative to hold the hockey stick with both hands while stopping with a puck on your stick. It is very difficult to do a sudden stop and control the puck if the stick is held with only one hand.

When practicing stops and starts, simulate a game situation where you have a breakaway opportunity. Prior to starting, remove your lower hand from the stick. Push the puck out ahead of you, swinging your arms for speed; angle your body well forward and try to take off exposively.

chapter 9

Turns and Transition for Multidirectional Moves

The ability to turn and change direction instantaneously is imperative in today's hockey. Players must be able to turn around without warning while maintaining or even gaining speed in the process.

A *turn* is the process of changing the body direction from facing forward to facing backward or from facing backward to facing forward. Turns may or may not involve a change in the direction of travel. For example, players often skate forward down the ice, turn around to face backward and skate backward down the ice in the same direction from which they came.

Transition (change) in hockey involves a change in the direction of travel but not necessarily a change from skating forward to skating backward or vice-versa. Transitions are some of the most exciting maneuvers to watch. The ability to transition quickly demands BAM—balance, agility, and maneuverability. Here is an example of a transitional situation. The play changes and the players must instantly respond and quickly move in a new direction.

Transitional situations may require

- a change from skating forward in one direction to skating backward in another (sometimes opposite) direction,
- a change from skating backward in one direction to skating forward in another (sometimes opposite) direction,
- a change from skating backward in one direction to skating backward in another, or
- a change from skating forward in one direction to skating forward in another (sometimes opposite) direction as with a pivot or tight turn. The pivot is a change of direction without *turning*. It is a spectacular and exciting maneuver that will be described later in this chapter.

Principles of Turns

Most, but not all, turns require a change of feet during the turn. All turns require an accompanying rotation of the entire body. When properly coordinated with a release of weight, the body rotation allows the player to switch from skating forward to backward or vice-versa. Like all skating maneuvers, turns are executed on the edges. Even turns that are done while skating on a straight line require the use of edges to provide traction in the ice.

The upper body and the hips must rotate to face the intended line of travel *before* turning or changing feet. The feet step around *after* the body has arrived. If you try to change feet before totally rotating your body, you will end up stepping sideways across the line of travel.

Turns require a release of body weight just prior to turning. Turns are actually mini-jumps. A scraping sound prior to turning indicates a snowplow. It is better to hop or jump into a turn than to scrape the ice.

To stay with or ahead of the action, speed must be maintained before and during the turn. After completing the turn players must accelerate. Novice players often put on the brakes (perform a snowplow skid) just before turning. This slows their speed and prevents them from turning quickly. As a result they are no longer able to stay with the play.

Finish each turn prepared to accelerate. Thrust powerfully and rapidly. Some players turn and coast. The idea is to turn and go! Otherwise you will be out of the play.

Turns are performed both skating on a straight line and on a curve or circle. When turning on a straight line, use slight edges. When turning on a curve or circle, use deeper edges. The deeper the edges and greater the knee bend, the sharper the curve.

Whether on the attack or on defense it is imperative to turn so that you face the action. Turning your back to the play limits your ability to see what is happening at the moment or to anticipate what the opponent is going to do next.

When turning on a curve or circle, the body rotation is sometimes in the same direction as the curve and sometimes in the opposite direction of the curve. Some turns require body rotation toward the center of the curve or circle and others require body rotation away from the center (this is the case when the turns are done on outside edges).

For example, when turning and changing from LFI to RBI, you travel a clockwise curve and your body rotates clockwise as well. When changing from RFI to LBI, you travel a counterclockwise curve, and your body rotates counterclockwise. But when turning and changing from LBI to RFI, you travel a counterclockwise curve, but your body rotates clockwise. And when turning and changing from RBI to LFI, you travel a clockwise curve while your body rotates counterclockwise.

You may also have to turn from backward to forward in the following ways: LBI to RFO, RBI to LFO, LBO to RFI, or RBO to LFI. In these four turns, the *direction of the curve* changes when you turn from backward to forward. These are more difficult turns that are used in transitional situations (change direction). Remember, the key factor in executing any turn is to turn your body (head, shoulders, chest, and hips) all the way around *before* changing feet or trying to step in the new direction!

Keep shoulders level, back straight, eyes and head up for all turns. If the leading shoulder drops or if you slump forward or put your head down, you may lose balance and speed. All players should try to master the turns and transitional maneuvers in this chapter. Practice all turns in both directions and give special attention to the weaker side. To practice a turn in the direction opposite the one described, mirror the instructions given.

Good position for going into a pivot. Mark Recchi skates deep edges, with his left leg beginning to perform the C-cut push.

Two-Foot Turns

These are the simplest turns to learn but are often used in game situations.

1. Turning from forward to backward. Glide forward on both skates. In preparation for turning, bend your knees deeply (90 degrees). At the moment you want to turn backward, quickly release your weight (like a mini-jump)

and simultaneously rotate your upper body (head, shoulders, and chest) and hips 180 degrees to face fully backward. Upon completing the turn immediately bend your knees again. You are now prepared to skate backward.

2. Turning from backward to forward. Glide backward on both skates. In preparation for turning, bend your knees deeply. At the moment you want to turn forward, quickly release your weight and simultaneously rotate your upper body (head, shoulders, and chest) and hips 180 degrees to face fully forward. Upon completing the turn immediately bend your knees again. You are now prepared to skate forward.

Turning From Forward to Backward on a Straight Line or Curve

I call this an *open turn,* or V *turn.* It is a two-step turn that involves changing feet during the turn. The directions given are for skating either on a straight line or curve and for turning to your right. If skating a straight line, use slight edges. If skating a curve or circle, use deeper edges. Remember to turn your head, shoulders, chest, and hips *before* turning and stepping onto the new gliding skate.

Step 1

1. Skate forward on the left inside edge. Hold your right skate and leg behind you and off the ice (figure 9.1a). Rotate your head, shoulders, chest, and hips clockwise (figure 9.1b).

2. Bring the free (right) skate close to the gliding (left) skate, turning the free skate to point backward (toe facing *opposite* the intended line of travel) as it draws near the gliding skate. The skates will be in an open, exaggerated V position, with heels close together and toes pointing in almost opposite directions (figure 9.1c). The right skate is still off the ice.

3. Keep rotating your head, shoulders, chest, and hips until your hips and the foot about to take the ice have turned 180 degrees to face fully backward. It is essential that the foot *about to* skate backward points backward (toe facing opposite the intended line of travel) before it takes the ice.

Remember: The skate cannot contact the ice facing backward unless your hips have already turned to face backward.

Step 2

1. Now change feet; place the right skate (slight inside edge) on the ice, lift the left skate, and skate backward. As you change feet, immediately lift the left skate (figure 9.1d). Otherwise it will be in the way of the right skate as it attempts to take the ice and you may trip yourself up.

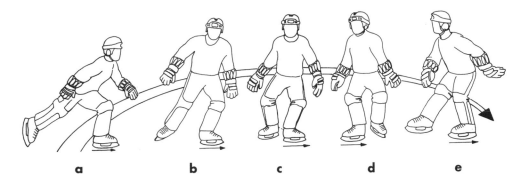

Figure 9.1 Turn from forward to backward on a straight line or curve.

2. You have completed the turn. The right skate is now the gliding skate and the left is the free skate. Thrust with the right leg, using the backward C-cut thrust against the inside edge of the right skate, and skate backward onto the left skate (figure 9.1e).

3. Execute a series of backward C-cut pushes and sprint backward.

Points to Remember

- Keep the skates close together in an exaggerated V-diamond position while switching them. If they are far apart, your weight will be split between them and the pushing skate will not be centered under your body. You will lose thrusting power and speed. A thrust is effective only when the body weight is totally over the thrusting skate.

- The use of slight inside edges is imperative when performing the turn. Without the edges to grip the ice, the pre-rotation of the upper body would also rotate the gliding skate, causing it to slide and scrape sideways on the ice.

- To execute this turn on a curve or circle, each skate must glide on a deep inside edge. Your body must rotate so that the chest faces toward the center of the curve.

Turning From Forward to Backward on a Curve With Chest Facing out of the Curve

Forward-to-backward turns are used in certain transitional situations. For example, let's say a defensive player skates forward into the team's offensive zone, but the opposing team gets the puck and the play changes. The defender must immediately turn from forward to backward in such a manner that he/she continues to face the play during the turn, then quickly retreat toward the defensive zone to prevent the opponent from breaking free.

This turn is executed on both skates and is done as a two-foot mini-jump. The chest faces out of the curve during the turn. It is described for turning clockwise or to your right (see figure 9.2).

1. Glide forward on both skates.
2. In preparation for turning, place 60 percent of your weight over the LFI of the outside skate and 40 percent over the RFO of the inside skate. Bend both knees deeply.

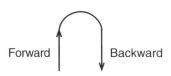

Forward   Backward

Figure 9.2 Turn from forward to backward with chest facing out of curve.

3. Release your weight and simultaneously rotate your entire body in a clockwise direction (to the right) until it faces fully backward.
4. Land skating backward with 60 percent of your weight over the LBI of the outside skate and 40 percent of your weight over the RBO of the inside skate

5. You have completed the turn. Do one left-over-right backward crossover, using the backward C-cut thrust against the LBI and the X push against the RBO.
6. Execute a series of backward C-cut pushes and sprint backward to the original starting point.

Turning From Backward to Forward on a Straight Line or Curve

There are two methods of executing this backward-to-forward turn. One employs the open (V) turn and the other employs a backward crossover prior to turning. Both can be performed on a straight line of travel (180 degrees) or on a curve or circle. Both variations should be practiced as straight-line and circle turns.

V or Open Turn

This is a two-step turn. It is described for skating on a straight line and for turning to your right.

Step 1

1. Skate backward, gliding on a slight LBI. Hold the right skate and leg in front of you (trailing your body) and off the ice (figure 9.3a).
2. Rotate your head, shoulders, chest, and hips clockwise—that is, to the right (figure 9.3b)—and bring the free (right) skate close to the gliding (left) skate, turning the free skate to point forward, toe facing the *intended* line of travel as it draws near the gliding skate. Your skates

will be in an open, exaggerated V-diamond position, with toes pointing in almost opposite directions (figure 9.3c). The right skate is still off the ice.

3. Keep rotating your head, shoulders, chest, and hips until your hips and free skate have turned 180 degrees to face fully forward, *toward the intended line of travel.* The right skate is still off the ice (figure 9.3d).

4. The toe of the skate about to take the ice *must* point forward along the intended line of travel before contacting the ice. But remember, the skate cannot contact the ice pointing forward until the hips have turned to face forward.

Step 2

1. To complete the turn, change feet; place the right skate (slight inside edge) on the ice, and skate forward (figure 9.3e).

2. As you step forward onto the right skate, push your left leg against the left inside edge, and accelerate (figure 9.3f). Sprint forward powerfully and quickly.

Points to Remember

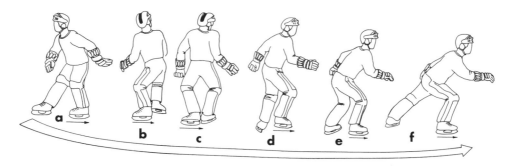

Figure 9.3 Turn from backward to forward (V or open turn) on a straight line or curve.

• Be sure that the skates are close together and in the exaggerated V-diamond position while changing feet. It is imperative that your body weight be totally concentrated and balanced over the pushing skate.

• The V-diamond position sets you up to accelerate out of the turn. Angle your body well forward and keep your weight toward the fronts of the inside edges (as though you were doing a front start; see chapter 7). Sprint forward.

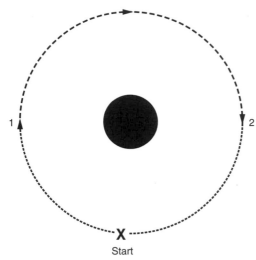

Figure 9.4 Turn from forward to backward on a circle—body rotates with chest facing toward center of circle: Skate forward on LFI from X; turn backward at 1; skate backward on RBI; turn forward at 2, skate forward on LFI to X.

• When executing this turn on a curve or circle, each skate must glide on a deep inside edge. The body must rotate so that chest faces the center of the curve. See figure 9.4 for a guide to forward and backward turns on a circle.

Backward Crossover Turn

This turn is described for skating on a clockwise circle or curve. Your upper body will rotate counterclockwise (to the left); your chest will face toward the center of the circle in preparation for turning. This is a three-step turn.

Step 1

a. Skate backward, gliding on the left outside edge. Hold the right skate and leg in front of you (trailing your body) and off the ice (figure 9.5a).

b. Prepare to do a backward crossover; start rotating your upper body and hips to the left.

Step 2

a. Do a right-over-left backward crossover. When the right skate takes the ice after crossing over, it skates backward on the RBI (figure 9.5, b-c).

b. While gliding backward on the RBI, continue rotating your head, shoulders, chest, and hips counterclockwise. Your chest will face toward the center of the curve as your body rotates (figure 9.5c).

c. Bring the free (left) skate close to the gliding (right) skate, and turn the free skate to point forward with toe facing the intended line of travel as it draws near the gliding skate. Your skates will be in the exaggerated V-diamond (almost spread-eagle) position. Note that the left skate is still off the ice (figure 9.5d).

d. Keep rotating your head, shoulders, chest, and hips until your hips and free skate have turned 180 degrees to face fully forward. It is essential that the toe of the free skate point forward before that skate takes the ice. Remember: the skate cannot point forward until your hips have fully turned forward.

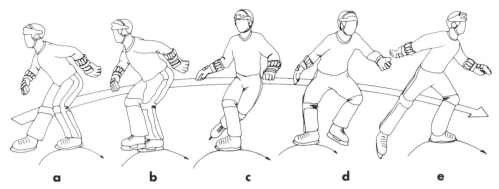

| a | b | c | d | e |

Figure 9.5 Turn from backward to forward using a backward crossover prior to turning.

Step 3

a. To complete the turn, change feet; place the left skate on the ice and skate forward onto the LFI (figure 9.5e). As you step onto the LFI, thrust the right leg against its inside edge.

b. The V-diamond position sets you up to accelerate out of the turn. Angle your body well forward and keep your weight toward the fronts of the inside edges as though you were doing a front start. Sprint forward powerfully and quickly.

Backward-to-forward turns are also used to transition (change direction). For example:

1. A defender backs up into the defensive zone, but the play suddenly changes and the puck is now controlled by a teammate. The defender must quickly change from skating backward to skating forward and charge in the opposite direction, toward the offensive zone.

2. Player backs up with the puck, waiting for an opportunity to change direction and skate forward toward the offensive zone.

3. Defender must accelerate after turning from backward to forward in order to cut off or check the attacking forward at the boards. I call this maneuver "diagonal transition."

See figure 9.6 for a guide to turning from backward to forward on a line diagonal to the original line of travel.

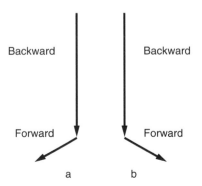

Figure 9.6 Turn from backward to forward on a diagonal line: (a) turning to left or (b) to right.

Points to Remember

- Use both pushes of the backward crossover to accelerate *into* the turn.
- Be sure the skates are close together and in the exaggerated V-diamond position just prior to changing feet. If the heels separate, your body weight will be split between your skates rather than concentrated and balanced over the thrusting skate, resulting in a loss of thrusting power.
- Keep knees bent and stay low while you turn. Straightening up throws your momentum upward, causing a loss of speed.
- While thrusting from backward to forward and during the initial forward strides, use the V-diamond position. Keep your body weight projected well forward, as in the front start, to accelerate.

Exercises for Improving Turns

The following exercises are only a few examples of the many available. They are divided into circle, straight-line, and pattern exercises. Mirror the instructions to practice turns in the opposite direction.

Circle Exercises

Exercise 1

1. Skate forward crossovers on a counterclockwise circle. Skate onto the RFI. Rotate your head, shoulders, chest, and hips counterclockwise 180 degrees, chest facing the center of the circle.
2. Turn backward onto the LBI.
3. With your left (outside) leg, thrust (backward C-cut push) against the inside edge of the left skate and do a series of left-over-right backward crossovers on the same counterclockwise circle.
4. On the last crossover, cross the left skate over in front of the right and skate onto the LBI. Pick up the right skate.
5. Rotate your head, shoulders, chest, and hips clockwise 180 degrees.
6. Turn forward and change feet, stepping onto the RFI.
7. Keep repeating the sequence, skating on a continuous circle of forward-to-backward and backward-to-forward turns.
8. Mirror the above exercise, skating clockwise.

Exercise 2

The first turn of this exercise requires body rotation with the chest facing away from the center of the circle, while the second turn requires body rotation with the chest facing toward it. A backward crossover is incorporated into the exercise.

1. Skate forward crossovers on a counterclockwise circle.
2. When your weight is on the LFO, rotate your head, shoulders, chest, and hips clockwise so that your chest faces away from the center of the circle. Turn backward, landing on both skates. This turn is like a mini-jump in that both feet come off the ice slightly to turn.
3. Thrust against the inside edge of your left (outside) skate (backward C-cut) and proceed to do a series of left-over-right backward crossovers on the same counterclockwise circle.
4. As you begin the last left-over-right crossover (don't forget to execute an X push) rotate your head, shoulders, chest, and hips clockwise toward the center of the circle. As you land on the LBI of the crossover, continue rotating your upper body clockwise (to the right) until it has turned 180 degrees to face fully forward.
5. Now step forward onto the RFI. Thrust the right skate and leg against the right inside edge and accelerate. Continue to accelerate, using right-over-left forward crossovers.
6. Repeat the sequence skating a continuous circle in the same direction.
7. Mirror the exercise skating in the opposite direction.

Exercise 3: Windmill

This exercise is described for skating on a counterclockwise circle. It is excellent for improving BAM (balance, agility, and mobility). The exercise consists of four steps performed with only one skate on the ice at a time. The body rotations are the same as for Exercise 2. To do the first turn, from forward to backward, rotate your body clockwise so that your chest faces *away* from the center of the circle. On the second turn, from backward to forward, continue to rotate your body clockwise. However, on this turn, the clockwise body rotation has your chest facing *toward* the center of the circle.

Step 1

1. Skate forward crossovers on a counterclockwise circle. Skate onto the LFO, holding the right skate and leg behind you and off the ice (figure 9.7a).
2. Rotate your head, shoulders, chest, and hips clockwise so that your chest faces away from the center of the circle. Continue to rotate your head, shoulders, chest, and hips and at the same time bring the free (right) skate behind the heel of the gliding (left) skate with the right heel facing backward, but still off the ice. The body must rotate 180 degrees to face fully backward and the heel of the free skate must fully

point toward the intended line of travel (backward) before the right skate takes the ice as the gliding skate.

Note: Make sure the right skate has room to pass behind the heel of the left skate in order to avoid a collision of the skates.

Step 2

1. Change feet. You are now skating on the RBO (figure 9.7b). Push with the left skate (driving against the left outside edge) as you change feet (figure 9.7c).

2. Keep rotating your upper body clockwise. As you rotate, your head, shoulders, chest, and hips will face toward the center of the circle.

Step 3

1. Do a left-over-right backward crossover. The left skate takes the ice on its LBI while the right leg thrusts (X push). After thrusting, the right leg becomes the free leg (figure 9.7, d-e).

2. Keep rotating your head, shoulders, chest, and hips until your body has turned to face fully forward. At the same time, bring the free (right) skate close to the gliding skate and turn it so that the toe points *forward* as it draws near the gliding skate. Your feet should now be in the exaggerated V-diamond position in preparation for stepping forward (figure 9.7f). The toe of the free skate must fully point toward the intended line of travel (forward) before it takes the ice as the new gliding skate.

Figure 9.7   Windmill exercise.

Step 4

1. Step forward onto the RFI. Thrust the left leg against the left inside edge as you step onto the right skate (figure 9.7g).

2. You have completed one sequence. To begin again, step onto the LFO and thrust against the inside edge of the right skate (figure 9.7a).

3. Continue the sequence by skating a continuous counterclockwise circle. Always rotate your body clockwise.

4. Mirror the exercise skating in the opposite direction.

As you become more proficient at this exercise, push harder, skate faster, and use deeper edges.

Figure 9.8 shows the pattern of the windmill exercise.

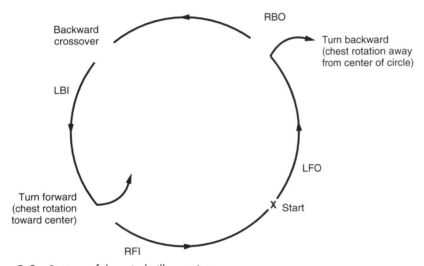

Figure 9.8 Pattern of the windmill exercise.

Straight-Line Exercises

Exercise 1

Sprint forward from the goal line. At the first blue line, turn backward (V turn), accelerate, and sprint backward to the center red line. At the red line, turn forward (V turn), accelerate, and sprint forward to the far blue line. At the far blue line, turn backward (open or V turn), accelerate, and sprint backward to the far goal line. Thrust and accelerate as you exit from each turn.

Note: Always turn your body toward the same sideboards of the rink. In this way your turns will be in one direction skating up the ice, and in the opposite direction coming back down the ice.

Variations

Try these variations:

1. Do the same exercise on whistle signals.
2. Do the same exercises on a straight line, using two-foot turns as described in Exercise 2 of the Circle Exercises (pages 160 and 161).

Exercise 2: Jump Turns

This exercise helps you to practice rotating your body 180 degrees and improve balance when recovering from situations that involve jumping.

1. Skate forward on a straight line.
2. On a whistle signal, jump up and turn around in the air a full 180 degrees. Land facing backward on both skates. Skate backward.
3. On the next whistle, jump up and turn around in the air a full 180 degrees. Land facing forward on both skates. Skate forward.

When landing, keep your back straight and knees bent to cushion the jolt, with the entire lengths of both blades in full contact with the ice. If the heels are off the ice, you will pitch forward over your toes.

Remember, you cannot turn around until your hips and upper body have fully turned (180 degrees).

Pattern Exercises

Exercise 1: N Drill

Refer to figure 8.16 (page 149), and perform turns at the Xs in the diagram.

1. Start in one corner of the rink and skate forward diagonally across the ice to the sideboards at the near blue line. At the sideboards turn backward (chest facing the endboards on your left). Do one backward crossover (right over left) and then skate backward across the ice and along the blue line to the sideboards. The turn from forward to backward is a two-foot turn with chest facing away from the center of the curve.

2. After skating backward across the ice, turn forward (chest facing the endboards on your right) and skate forward diagonally across the ice to the sideboards at the center red line. The turn from backward to forward is a left-over-right backward crossover turn with chest facing toward the

center of the curve. Do not decelerate before or during the turn; accelerate upon exiting from it.

3. When you reach the sideboards at the center red line, turn backward facing the endboards on your left (two-foot turn with body facing out of the curve) and skate backward across the ice along the red line to the sideboards.

4. At the sideboards, turn forward (left over right backward crossover turn) facing the endboards on your right and skate forward diagonally across the ice to the far blue line.

5. When you reach the sideboards at the blue line, turn backward facing the endboards on your left (two-foot turn with body facing out of the curve). Do one right-over-left backward crossover and skate backward across the ice along the blue line to the sideboards.

6. At the opposite sideboards, turn forward (left over right backward crossover turn) and skate forward diagonally across the ice to the goal line.

7. When you reach the goal line, turn backward (two-foot turn with body facing out of the curve). Do one right over left backward crossover and skate backward along the goal line to the new starting position (figure 8.16).

8. Repeat with all turns facing the same sideboards; the turns will now be executed in the other direction (right as opposed to left, or vice versa).

Remember: The two-foot turn is done like a mini-jump. The jumping action releases your body weight. This is necessary for a quick and smooth turn.

Exercise 2: Turn Exercise

This exercise is diagrammed in figure 9.9. Be sure to accelerate when exiting from all turns.

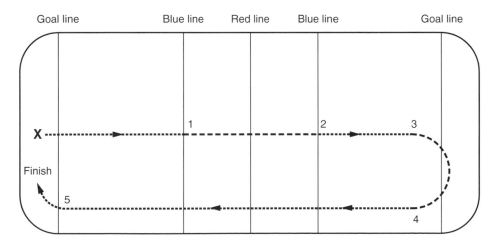

Figure 9.9 Turn exercise.

1. Start from the goal line. Skate forward to the first blue line (1) and turn, facing one predetermined sideboards. Skate backward to the far blue line (2).

2. At the far blue line, turn, facing the same sideboards, and skate forward to the end face-off circle (3). From there, turn backward, facing the goal crease; immediately execute one backward crossover and then turn forward (4). Skate forward, returning back up the ice to point 5.

3. Repeat the exercise with all turns facing the other sideboards in order to practice turning the other way.

Exercise 3: Turns Along the Blue Line

In this exercise only one skate is on the ice at any time and the upper body stays *parallel* (sideways) to the line of travel throughout. The exercise entails continuous turns from forward to backward and from backward to forward, turning 180 degrees and changing feet *as quickly as possible.* The upper body must face the same end of the rink throughout.

1. Start from one sideboard at the blue line. Glide forward along the blue line on the left skate with the right skate off the ice and behind you. Rotate your upper body so that your head, shoulders, and chest face the goal line to your right.

2. Change feet and glide backward on the right skate (still along the blue line) for a very short distance. Keep the left skate off the ice and behind you, upper body facing the same goal line.

3. Change feet to glide forward along the blue line on the left skate again for a very short distance, keeping the right skate off the ice. Maintain the same upper-body position.

4. Keep turning and changing feet—left skate on the ice when gliding forward and right skate on the ice when gliding backward—until you reach the opposite sideboards.

It may help to do this exercise while holding a hockey stick horizontally in both hands. Keep the stick *parallel* to the goal line you are facing. This will assist in keeping your upper body sideways to the line of travel.

Be sure to push from one skate to the other instead of just stepping. Remember that to push, you must use the edges, bend your knees, and keep your body weight concentrated over the thrusting leg.

Repeat the drill, now gliding forward on the right skate and backward on the left.

Defensive Turn Exercises

In every hockey game, defenders face forwards who are racing along the boards with the puck, looking for an opportunity to pass to a teammate or to move into scoring position. The next three exercises simulate these situations—the defender is skating backward and tracking the forward, but at a certain point must quickly turn, skate forward, and cut off the attacking player. Sometimes the defender cuts off the opponent at the sideboards and sometimes in open ice.

Exercise 1

Start backward from the goal line using a backward crossover start, and skate straight backward using C-cuts to the first blue line.

At the blue line, turn forward (V turn), facing the sideboards to your left. As soon as you have turned forward, accelerate by thrusting as in the front start (V-diamond position) and sprint forward on a diagonal path to reach the sideboards at the center red line (figure 9.10, a-c).

Repeat the exercise, this time turning to face the sideboards to your right.

c   b   a

Figure 9.10 Turn from backward to forward (V turn) to cut off an opponent to the left.

Exercise 2

This exercise is described for turning from backward to forward to your right. Start in the same manner as in Exercise 1. This time when you reach the first blue line use a backward crossover preceding the turn from backward to forward, then turn forward facing the sideboards to your right. As soon as you have turned forward, accelerate by thrusting as in the front start, and sprint forward on a diagonal path to reach the sideboards at the center red line (figure 9.11, a-g).

Repeat the exercise, this time turning to face the sideboards to your left.

Figure 9.11 Turn from backward to forward (using backward crossover turn) to cut off an opponent.

Exercise 3

Start in the same manner as described in Exercise 1 and skate straight backward to the first blue line.

At the blue line, turn forward 180 degrees using the open V turn and skate forward along the same straight line of travel. After the turn, accelerate by thrusting as in the front start. Sprint the length of the ice. Alternate the turning side on each repetition.

Exercise 4

Repeat Exercise 3, but use a backward crossover prior to turning from backward to forward. Be sure to use both pushes of the backward crossover to accelerate into the turn.

Exercises for Transition

Transition From Skating Forward in One Direction to Skating Backward in the Opposite Direction

The In-Out Drill

1. Start forward from one sideboards using the front start. Skate at full speed to center ice (see figure 9.12).

2. At center ice turn backward to your left, chest facing out of the circle. Do one backward crossover (right over left), and skate straight backward (backward C-cuts) to your starting point at the sideboards. Stop, using a backward snowplow stop.

3. Repeat steps 1 and 2, now turning backward to your right and doing a left-over-right backward crossover.

Note: Do not slow down (by scraping the ice or stopping) prior to turning from forward to backward. Learn how to accelerate as you transition into the new direction.

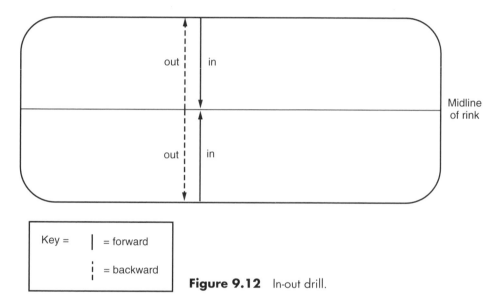

Figure 9.12 In-out drill.

Transition From Skating Backward In One Direction to Skating Forward in the Opposite Direction

The U Drill

This exercise is described for transitioning and turning to the right (clockwise).

1. Start backward at the goal line with a backward crossover start and skate using backward C-cuts to the near blue line (figure 9.13).

Entering into the transition:

2. At the blue line pick up the right skate and glide backward on the inside edge of the left skate (LBI). Dig the inside deeply into the ice and bend the left knee deeply. Balance over the left skate, keeping heels and knees in the V-diamond position. The deep inside edge will curve sharply to the right (clockwise).

Exiting from the transition:

3. At precisely the midpoint of the curve, thrust the left leg against the LBI, and change feet so that you are now skating forward on the inside edge of the right skate (RFI). The combination of LBI and RFI create a U-shaped pattern in the ice. Try to keep the U as tight as possible as you turn from backward to forward.

4. Sprint forward to the goal line from which you started.

5. Repeat, now turning from backward to forward to the left (counterclockwise). You will transition from the RBI to the LFI.

Repeat the U drill, but now use a backward crossover prior to the transitional move (backward inside edge to forward inside edge).

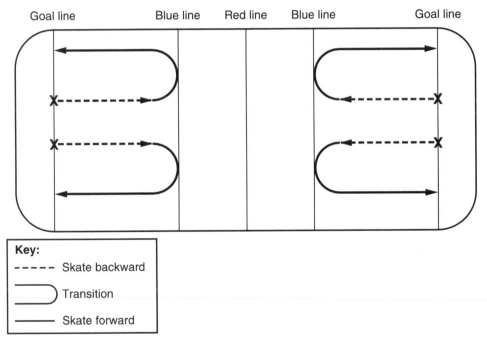

Figure 9.13 U drill.

The Total Transition Drill

This exercise combines forward-to-backward transitions with backward-to-forward transitions. Do not stop or slow down during any of the transitional turns. The exercise is described for turning to the sideboards on your left.

1. Do a front start from one goal line and skate forward to the far blue line (figure 9.14).

2. At the far blue line quickly turn to your left (chest facing out of the circle), do a powerful backward crossover (right over left), and skate backward (C-cuts) in the direction from which you came, until you reach the near blue line.

3. At the near blue line turn to your left (clockwise) using the method described in the U Drill (transition from RBI to LFI) and sprint forward until you reach the goal line on the far end of the ice. You have completed one sequence.

4. Repeat the drill, now always turning to face the sideboards on your right.

Do not slow down or stop at any time. Try to make all transitions fast and powerful and smooth.

Variations

- You can also practice this drill by turning at each line—for example, skate forward from goal line to center red line, backward to first blue line, forward to second blue line, backward to center red line, and forward down the length of the ice.

- Alternate the direction of turning during the drill. For example, do one set of backward and forward turns facing the sideboards on your left; do the next set of backward and forward turns facing the sideboards on your right.

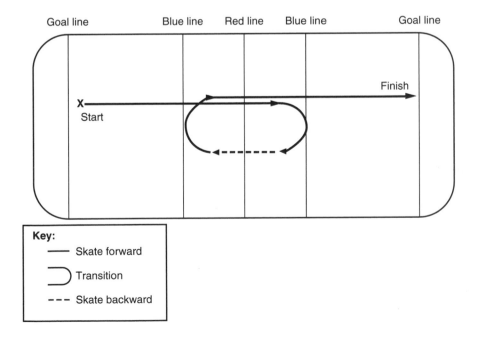

Figure 9.14 Total transition drill.

The Z Drill

All turns in this drill should face the sideboards to your left.

1. Start backward from the corner of the rink as shown in figure 9.15, and take two or three rapid backward strides.

2. After the second or third stride (when you are gliding on the right skate) pick up the left skate and quickly bring it into the V-diamond position with the gliding skate.

3. Turn forward and take two or three rapid strides forward. Turn backward (chest facing out of curve) and take two or three rapid strides backward.

4. Keep repeating this sequence until you have reached the far corner of the rink, diagonally across from where you started.

5. Change the corner you start from—all turns should now face the sideboards to your right.

All turns and transitional moves should be practiced slowly at first, then faster and faster. Practice them without the puck at first, then while controlling a puck at top speed.

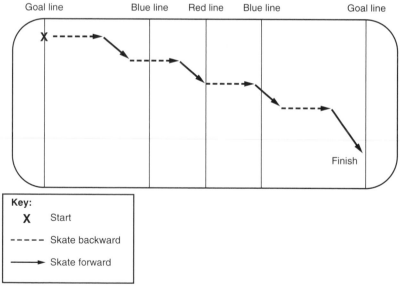

Figure 9.15 Z drill.

The Pivot or Tight Turn

Wayne Gretzky was and remains the master of the pivot. He used it almost magically, and always to his advantage. The pivot is a forward skating move in which the player executes a tight turn and emerges from it *still skating forward*, but in a new direction (figure 9.16). It is an extremely important hockey move because it gives the player numerous options. It is also one of the most effective moves when trying to elude an opponent. In this instance, the attacking player wards off the opposition with one shoulder and arm while protecting the puck trying to push around and beyond the reach of the defender ("bulling").

The pivot consists of two equally divided phases: the entry and the exit. The move requires very deep knee bend and edges on both the

Figure 9.16 The pivot or tight turn.

gliding and pushing legs, with proper weight distribution over the skates and proper upper body positioning for balance.

The entry phase of the pivot is done with both skates on the ice. The inside skate glides on a deep outside edge while the outside skate and leg execute a C-cut push against the inside edge. The C-cut push provides acceleration into and through the first half of the pivot. The depth of the edges and the downward pressure of the body weight over them determine the sharpness of the pivot.

The tighter the pivot, the more important it is to keep the body weight over the back halves of the blades on the entry phase. Weight on the front halves causes the blades to skid instead of cutting into the ice.

The exit phase requires a powerful and rapid crossover (with the accompanying X push) in order to accelerate from the pivot.

When executing a pivot, keep your shoulders level to the ice. It is often necessary to keep the inside shoulder slightly higher than the outside shoulder as this provides even greater stability. Lowering (dropping) the inside shoulder causes a lean or tilt into the circle, which at speed and on a sharp curve causes a loss of balance.

The pivot is described for curving to the left (counterclockwise). Skate forward to a pylon and prepare to pivot around it in a counterclockwise direction (figure 9.17a).

Phase 1: The Entry

1. At the pylon, dig in the edges of both skates and bend your knees deeply. The inside (left) skate is on a strong outside edge and the outside (right) skate is on a strong inside edge. Your body weight must be concentrated above the outside skate in preparation for pushing.

2. Thrust the outside (right) skate and leg against the inside edge (C-cut push) and simultaneously glide on a deep LFO in order to turn sharply around the pylon. Thrust with the back half of the inside edge. During the push, transfer your weight onto the LFO of the gliding skate. Figure 9.17b demonstrates step 1 performed with the chest facing into the curve; 9.17c demonstrates step 1 with the chest facing out of the curve.

a b c

d e f

Figure 9.17 The pivot: *(a)* preparation; *(b)* entry: chest faces toward or *(c)* away from center of curve; *(d)* reaching apex of the pivot, hips continuously face direction of travel; *(e)* exit from pivot with crossover; *(f)* skate forward.

3. Keep your hips continuously facing into the circular direction of travel during the maneuver (figure 9.17d). If the hips don't turn continuously, you can't pivot quickly.

Phase 2: The Exit

1. At the *midpoint* of the pivot do a right-over-left crossover and push the left leg (X push) against its outside edge. The X push provides acceleration on the exit phase of the pivot (figure 9.17e). If it is omitted or only partially utilized you will be unable to exit at speed. Execute the X push powerfully and quickly. Land the crossover on the front part of the right inside edge in order to accelerate quickly.

2. Emerge from the pivot skating forward either toward the direction from which you came or in a new direction (figure 9.17f).

3. Practice the pivot in the opposite (clockwise) direction. The right skate is now the inside skate and glides on its outside edge. The left skate is now the outside skate and cuts the C-cut push against its inside edge.

The pivot can be done either with the outside shoulder leading and your chest facing toward the center of the circle (figure 9.17b) or with the inside shoulder leading and your chest facing away from the center of the circle (figure 9.17c). Practice both positions. Regardless of the position, shoulders must be held level with the ice (or with the inside shoulder held slightly higher than the outside shoulder).

The pivot can be used as a full-circle (360-degree) turn, a three-quarter-circle (270-degree) turn, a half-circle (180-degree) turn, or any part of a circle the situation demands. Players who master this maneuver gain great maneuverability.

Pivot Exercises

When performing pivot exercises, hold the hockey stick with both hands. Keep the stick blade on the ice in order to control a puck during pivot maneuvers. Practice pivot exercises first without a puck, then with it.

Exercise 1

Pivot 360 degrees around a series of pylons. After pivoting halfway around each pylon, execute a crossover (and the accompanying X push). Accelerate through the exit phase of the pivot. Skate to the next pylon and pivot around it in the opposite direction. Alternate the direction of the pivot at each pylon and stay as close to each pylon as possible (figure 9.18).

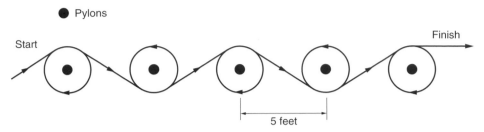

Figure 9.18 360-degree pivots around pylons.

Exercise 2

Practice 270-degree pivots around a pylon. Skate forward and pivot 270 degrees around a pylon. After the pivot, skate back in the opposite direction from which you came. At the midpoint of the pivot, do one crossover and accelerate out of the pivot.

Exercise 3

Set up pylons and practice 270-degree pivots in figure-eight patterns (figure 9.19).

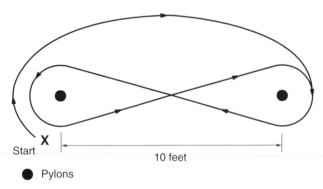

Figure 9.19 Figure-eight pivots around pylons.

Exercise 4

Sprint forward from the goal line, staying just to the left of the midline of the rink. Just before reaching the center red line, pivot toward the sideboards on your left. *Do not* cross the midline of the rink prior to pivoting. *Stay inside* (toward the center of the ice) the face-off dots on the left side of the rink as you pivot, cross over, and skate forward to your starting place (figure 9.20).

Repeat the drill, now starting just to the right of the midline of the rink and pivoting toward the sideboards on your right.

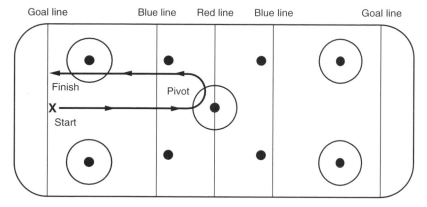

Figure 9.20 Pivot exercise.

Exercise 5

Follow the N pattern diagrammed in figure 8.16 (page 149) for an additional pivot drill. Skate forward from a corner of the rink and follow the pattern, pivoting at each X. Be sure to complete each pivot with a crossover. Practice pivoting in both directions.

Exercise 6

This is a combination two-foot turn, pivot exercise. It simulates a game situation in which a player backs up with the puck. The player is being chased by an opposing player and wants to avoid losing the puck.

1. Pair up with a partner. You will act as the player and will skate backward with the puck. Your partner will act as the opposing player and will skate forward, trying to catch you and capture the puck.

2. When your partner is about six feet away from you, do a two-foot turn (from backward to forward). Now execute a pivot (C-cut and X pushes) and accelerate in another direction to escape from your partner.

There are many variations and patterns for practicing pivots. The better the skater, the more challenging the drills should be.

Points to Remember

- Keep pivots as tight as possible.
- Knee bend, edge depth, hip and upper-body rotation, and speed determine the tightness of the pivot.
- Keep the inside shoulder slightly higher than the outside shoulder. This balance factor increases in importance with speed and depth of curve.

Exercise 7: "Bulling" Around an Opposing Player

This is one of Jaromir Jagr's greatest moves: As he drives to get into scoring position, the defending player leans on him, attempting to push him toward the boards, and at the same time trying to steal the puck. Jagr counters by pushing against the defender (with his inside arm and shoulder) while protecting the puck and doing a variation of the pivot to cut around the defender ("bulling").

To practice this maneuver, team up with another player. One acts as the attacker, the other as the defender. The forward stays to the outside of the defender.

Skate forward to the far blue line, staying abreast of each other. At the blue line the defender should lean on the attacker with his or her shoulder and attempt to push the attacker toward the boards.

To counter, the attacker should try to cut around the defender. In this situation the attacker needs to put his or her back to (and face away) from the defender. The inside shoulder must be high and leading. The upper body must be positioned so the chest faces away from the center of the curve and away from the defender (figure 9.21).

The attacker uses the inside shoulder, arm, and back muscles to push against the defender while executing several continuous C-cuts. Deep edges and strong C-cut thrusts with the outside leg are essential.

The attacker's goal is to use this variation of the pivot for power and stability while trying to gain a lead on and cut around the defender. As soon as the attacker gains the slightest lead, he or she executes a powerful and quick crossover to cut in front of and escape from the defender.

Keep the inside shoulder higher than the outside shoulder throughout the pivot. If you lower it, the defender will be able to pull you (the attacker) down. This is especially true

Figure 9.21 Bulling around an opposing player.

when traveling at a high speed. If you tilt into the circle just a bit too much, the defender has only to back away for you (the attacker) to land on the ice!

Now practice bulling while holding the hockey stick with just the top hand and still protecting the puck as you bull around the defender.

As with all hockey moves, practice slowly at first and then with increasing leg speed until you can perform correctly, powerfully, and quickly, with and without the puck.

chapter 10

Agility for Maximum Coverage of the Ice

If you remember how Wayne Gretzky skated in, around, and through the opposition, you will understand the importance of agility on the ice. Agility often marks the difference between a mediocre hockey player and a star. It allows a player to outfox an opponent or keep a foe at bay, and to execute a wide range of moves with dazzling speed and mobility. Agile hockey players can regain their feet and get back into the play quickly after a fall or unexpected body check. They seem to be everywhere; they dominate the action.

The skills and exercises in this chapter are designed to improve agility. Goalies also should concentrate on improving agility—it is key to success in the nets.

Several maneuvers already covered in this book can also be categorized as agility maneuvers—for example, crossovers, turns, transitional moves, and pivots.

As always, practice all agility maneuvers slowly at first, then faster and faster, without a puck, then while controlling a puck.

Exercises for Improving Agility

360-Degree Spin-Around

Hard checks can send players reeling to the ice. Some skaters manage to stay on their feet and retain their composure after such checks, while others end up out of the play. This exercise simulates such a situation. By practicing it your balance and recovery times from these situations will improve.

The spin-around involves making a 360-degree rotation as rapidly as possible. It is executed with both skates on the ice during the spin.

1. Skate forward. Pretend you've just been hit with a hard check to your shoulder that spins you around completely so that after the spin you are facing forward again.

2. When spinning, stay on the flats of the blades with your weight on the balls of your feet. Do not try to dig in the edges to spin around. If the edges catch the ice you will have difficulty making a rapid spin.

3. Although the turn is actually a combination of two turns (a forward-to-backward turn and a backward-to-forward turn) try to spin around in one continuous motion.

4. The immediate concern after coming out of the spin is to get back into the play. This requires rapid acceleration. When you complete the spin-around and are facing forward again, dig into the ice with the inside edge of the back (pushing) skate, thrust powerfully with the back leg and sprint back to the action.

5. Keep the hockey stick on or close to the ice as you spin around. Holding the stick with both hands, bring the stick around with you so it remains in front of you and close to the ice as you exit from the spin. A need to swing the stick high into the air as you spin is a sign of poor upper-body control and lack of stability. It also raises your center of gravity. These factors affect balance, speed, and recovery time.

Practice the 360-degree spin-around in both directions.

Variation

Practice spinning around on whistle signals. On the first signal, spin around 360 degrees in one direction. On the next whistle, spin in the other direction. Alternate directions to develop both rotations and to avoid dizziness. The drill can also be done spinning around at the near blue line, center red line, and far blue line.

Inside Edges Around Pylons

When performing this exercise, use each skate and leg first to glide (for curved direction) and then to thrust (for acceleration). Refer to figure 10.1.

1. Start from one corner of the rink and skate forward to the first pylon. At the pylon, curve around it by gliding on the inside edge (45-degree angle) of the outside skate. The knee of the gliding skate must be bent deeply (90 degrees). Keep your back straight, eyes and head up. Keep the other skate (the inside skate) off the ice and close to the gliding skate with skates and knees in the V-diamond position.

2. After curving halfway around the pylon, the gliding skate becomes the pushing skate. Thrust the pushing leg against the inside edge on which you have been gliding to accelerate from the glide and sprint forward to

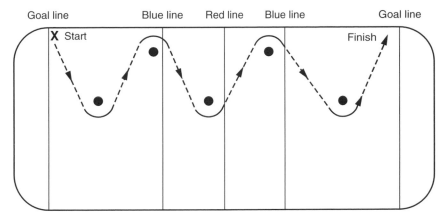

Figure 10.1   Edges around pylons.

the next pylon. Again, curve around the pylon by gliding on the inside edge of the outside skate with the inside skate off the ice and close to the gliding skate, skates and knees in the V-diamond position.

3. After curving halfway around the pylon, thrust the pushing leg against the inside edge on which you have been gliding. Sprint forward to the next pylon.

4. Continue skating to and curving around each pylon until you reach the opposite corner of the rink.

5. Repeat, skating backward. Each push is now the backward C-cut push.

Outside Edges Around Pylons

Perform the previous exercise forward and backward, but now curve half-way around each pylon, gliding on the outside edge of the inside skate. Keep the outside skate off the ice. At this point, thrust against the outside edge of the skate on which you have been gliding (X push) and do a crossover. The outside skate, after crossing over, takes the ice on its inside edge.

Note: Be sure to use the X push to accelerate from each crossover. Sprint from one pylon to the next.

Backward-to-Forward Turns Around Pylons

Skate the same pattern as in the previous exercises. Start out and skate backward to the first pylon. Curve backward halfway around it on the inside edge of the outside skate. Then turn forward quickly, thrust the pushing leg against the inside edge on which you've been gliding and take two rapid forward strides toward the next pylon. After the second stride turn backward quickly and skate backward to the next pylon. Curve halfway around it on the inside edge of the outside skate. At this point turn forward quickly, thrust the pushing leg against the inside edge on which you've been gliding, and take two rapid forward strides toward the next pylon. After the second stride, turn backward quickly and skate backward to the next pylon. Continue this exercise until you reach the opposite corner of the rink.

All backward-to-forward turns will have the body rotation with chest facing toward the center of the curve (facing the pylons).

As you curve around each pylon, keep the inside skate off the ice, close to the gliding skate with skates and knees in the V-diamond position.

Many variations of the previous drills may be designed, incorporating spin-arounds, forward-to-backward and backward-to-forward turns, full circles around pylons, and so on.

Knee Drops

Players often fall or drop to their knees to block shots. They must be able to quickly return to an upright position and resume skating rapidly to stay with the action. Be sure to drop gently so as not to injure your knees. *Those with knee problems should not do knee drops.*

Keep your back straight and head up throughout this exercise.

1. Stand in place on the ice. Hold a hockey stick horizontally at chest height in front of you, arms outstretched. Keep the stick in this position during the entire drill. At no time should your hands, elbows, or stick touch the ice.
2. On a whistle signal, drop to both knees (figure 10.2a).
3. On a second whistle, sit down to one side of your skates (figure 10.2b). Be sure to practice sitting both ways. Here, too, most skaters favor one side over the other.
4. On a third whistle, get up on both knees (see figure 10.2a). On a fourth whistle, get back up on your feet.

Variations

1. On the first whistle, drop to both knees simultaneously. On the next whistle, get up on your feet. Keep repeating as rapidly as possible.
2. Skate forward or backward down the ice. On the first whistle, drop to both knees just as you did in the previous variation. On the second whistle, get back up on your feet and get back into stride as quickly as possible.
3. Skate forward or backward down the ice. On the first whistle, drop to one knee, and on the second whistle get back up on your feet. Keep repeating this on alternating knees (figure 10.2c).

4. Skate forward. On the whistle, drop to both knees. On the next whistle, get up, immediately turn backward, and skate backward rapidly. On the next whistle, drop to both knees. On the next whistle, get up, immediately turn forward, and skate forward rapidly. This exercise can also be done dropping onto one knee. Alternate knees.

Points to Remember

- At no time should hands, elbows, or stick touch the ice.
- When preparing to get up, center the support skate *directly underneath your body* with the entire blade length flat against the ice (see figure 10.2c). If you place only the front toe of the blade on the ice and lift your heel off the ice, you will not be able to get up (figure 10.2d).

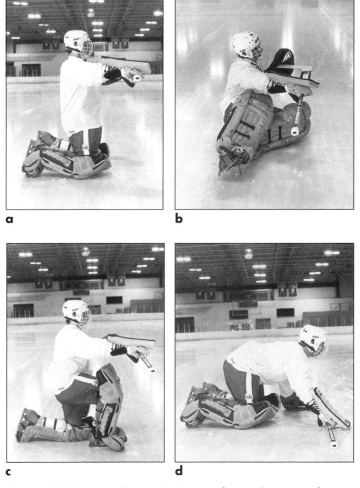

Figure 10.2 Knee drops: *(a-c)* correct form; *(d)* incorrect form.

- Keep your back straight with your eyes and head up at all times. If your shoulders and head slump forward, your weight will pitch over you toes and you will not be able to get up.

Jaromir Jagr skates with agility and balance. Here he is shown skating on his inside edge: knee is well-bent, feet are close together, and his stick is on the ice.

Jumps Over Hockey Sticks

The ability to be airborne, land on one or both skates, and then sprint without losing speed is an example of agility. You never know when you will be thrown into the air by an unexpected body check or have to jump over a fallen player.

The ability to land and resume skating without breaking stride requires balance, body control, power, and stability. The use of the knees as shock absorbers is critical.

The following exercises are designed to improve balance and recovery capabilities in such situations.

1. Place a hockey stick horizontally over two pylons, the height of which is dependent on the size and ability of the skater.

2. Skate forward. Approach the stick gliding on two feet. Take off from both skates, lifting both knees simultaneously, and jump over the stick. Land on both skates with both blades in full contact with the ice. If the heels are off the ice as you land, you will end up on the curved toes of the skates and may fall forward. If you land with your weight too far back over the heels, you may fall backward. On landing, flex both knees deeply and keep your back straight, shoulders back, eyes and head up. Advanced skaters can jump over the stick while skating backward. Even more advanced skaters can try this variation: skate forward, jump over the stick, turn 180 degrees in the air, land backward, and immediately sprint without losing stride. Very advanced skaters may try to jump and turn 360 degrees in the air.

3. Do the previous exercise, now leaping over the stick. Take off from one skate and land on the other. Drive off with the back leg. Land on the opposite skate, keeping the takeoff skate off the ice. Your body weight should be on the middle of the landing blade. Advanced skaters can turn in the air and land backward on the other skate, or jump and land on the same skate (forward or backward).

To get the height necessary for clearing the stick, you must push your body into the air. Drive the thrusting leg powerfully and fully. Do not slow down prior to jumping. You will acquire more height and clearance by accelerating into the takeoff. Immediately after landing, resume skating rapidly, trying not to break stride.

Lateral Crossover Leaps

A player skating forward or backward on a straight line who wants to make a sudden sideways move toward the boards or leap sideways over a fallen player may have to execute a lateral crossover leap. The move is similar to a crossover start.

This exercise is similar to the side start exercise performed over hockey sticks (chapter 7) except that only one stick is used.

1. Place a hockey stick horizontally on top of two pylons, parallel to the direction of travel rather than perpendicular to it. The height of the stick from the ice is dependent on the size and ability of the skater.

2. Skate forward until you are alongside and to the right of the stick.

3. Leap over the stick by doing a lateral crossover. Drive the inside (left) leg against its outside edge (X push) to provide thrust through the leap, while simultaneously crossing the outside (right) leg over the left. Drive the crossing (right) knee and your body weight sideways (to the left).

4. Leap over the stick. The right skate should land on the other side of the stick and on its inside edge, with the skate blade almost parallel to the stick (figure 10.3a-b).

5. As soon as you land, pivot fully forward and use strong and rapid pushes to accelerate and sprint forward (see figure 10.3c).

6. Do the exercise leaping over the stick from the other side (left-over-right crossover). Very advanced skaters can try the same from a backward skating position. When doing this, the leap will be a backward lateral crossover.

a   b   c

Figure 10.3 Lateral crossover leap over stick.

Dives

Hockey players quickly learn to expect the unexpected. You never know when you'll take a dive on the ice, but sooner or later you will. When it happens, you must be able to get to your feet quickly and immediately return to the action. Practicing these exercises will improve your ability to recover quickly from such falls.

1. Place a hockey stick horizontally on top of two pylons. Skate forward rapidly.

2. At the stick, belly flop with your hands flat out and your feet outstretched behind you and on the ice. Keep your head up as you belly flop. Dive under the stick, trying not to knock it down.

3. After passing under the stick, get up as quickly as possible and resume skating with speed.

Variation

Combine jumps and dives. Practicing them will improve the agility and quickness needed to jump up, land on your feet, dive, recover, and get back into stride with as little loss of time as possible.

Design a challenging pylon course. It is particularly difficult to dive, recover quickly, and leap over another stick that is only a few feet away from the stick under which you have just dived.

Defending Against a Check

Why can some hockey players remain in front of the net and withstand body checks that would stun other players? The answer lies in their ability to apply the principles of edges, knee bend, and body weight to get maximum grip into the ice. Many players are unable to withstand checks because they do not have enough traction to provide stability. In hockey, once you've gotten to your desired position, you must stay on your feet and hold your ground.

As always, the more you dig in the edges and bend your knees, the more stable—and therefore stronger—you become. To push against a checking player, press down into the ice with as much knee bend as possible and with the maximum grip and leg drive you can apply to the *inside* edges. One of the most common errors is straightening up as you are being checked. This pulls your edges, knees, and center of gravity up and causes you to lean away from the check. The result of this is usually a fall.

If you are the player delivering the check, you need the same stability. You must also use the inside edges, knees, leg drive, and body weight to effectively push against the opposing player. Without them, you will more than likely bounce off your opponent rather than taking him or her out of the play. A proper check works from the skates up. Check first with the edges, then the knees, the legs, and the hips. Finish the check by pushing against the opponent with the upper body (chest and shoulder).

1. Work with a partner. Each of you should lean on (check) the other, shoulder to shoulder.

2. Both players must dig into the ice with the inside edge of the outside (back) skate. With body weight over that skate, thrust against the inside edge of that skate. Try to move each other without giving up ice. If you cannot stand your ground, you are not digging in with enough inside edge, knee bend, or body weight. Strength on the ice depends on more than just size.

Tracking the Opponent

Pair up with another skater. Begin by skating as a forward while your partner acts as a defender. Use crossover steps and leaps in alternating lateral directions, trying to "deke" (fake) the defender. The defender should track you by mirroring and following your every move. Whichever way you go, the defender must also go. Reverse roles and repeat the drill.

Now do this exercise with one of you skating straight forward and the other skating straight backward. At a moment's notice, the forward should make a move laterally. The defender must immediately respond (figure 10.4 a and b).

a

b

Figure 10.4 Tracking the opponent.

Signal Drill

This drill combines many different skating skills, each performed in an unannounced sequence. The purpose is to develop agility and instantaneous response.

A particular signal will indicate a corresponding maneuver. On that signal, perform that maneuver as quickly as possible. The moves will be done one after the other with no warning as to which will follow. A typical sequence might be as follows:

1. Skate forward.
2. Do crossover leaps to the right.
3. Skate backward.
4. Do crossover leaps to the left.
5. Pivot (tight turn) 360 degrees to the right.
6. Skate forward.
7. Drop to your knees and get up.
8. Skate backward, drop to your knees, and get up.
9. Pivot (tight turn) 360 degrees to the left.
10. Skate forward and stop.
11. Drop to your knees, belly flop, get up on your knees, and get up on your feet.
12. Skate forward, spin around 360 degrees, and continue skating forward without breaking stride.

The variations on this drill are endless. The drill is excellent for working on technique, and is also fun. Try a game of follow the leader using some of the variations.

Maneuvering the Puck With Your Skates

To the astonishment of fans, hockey players control the puck as easily with their skates as they do with their hockey sticks. To develop this skill, skate without a stick and control the puck with your skates. Try to move the puck from skate to skate. Don't kick it out in front of you. Keep your eyes and head up; do not look down at the puck.

Other ways to develop this skill, using a puck but no sticks, include playing one-on-one with another player, free-for-all with several players, or even a regular game with fully equipped goalies. Remember, everyone has only skates for shooting, passing, and puck control—no sticks!

Additional Agility Drills

Exercise 1

The tightness of the pattern in this exercise requires deep edges, body control, and agility. Skate rapidly throughout. Refer to figure 10.5.

1. Start at X; sprint forward to point 1.
2. At 1, turn backward, chest facing into the circle. Perform backward crossovers, left over right, to point 2.
3. Between 2 and 3, sprint backward (backward C-cuts).
4. From 3 to 4, perform backward crossovers, left over right.
5. At 4, turn forward, chest facing into the circle.
6. From 4 to 1, sprint forward (forward stride).

Variations

1. Skate forward and use forward crossovers only.
2. Skate backward and use backward crossovers only.
3. Turn at 1, chest facing outside instead of facing inside the circle.

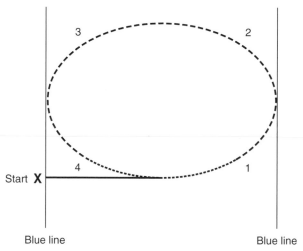

Figure 10.5 Agility exercise 1.

Exercise 2

Refer to figure 10.6.

1. Sprint forward from X to 1.
2. Turn backward at 1 and skate backward to point 2, using backward crossovers.
3. Turn forward at 2 and skate forward to point 3, using forward crossovers.
4. Turn backward at 3 and skate backward to point 4.
5. At point 4, turn forward and skate to X, using forward crossovers.

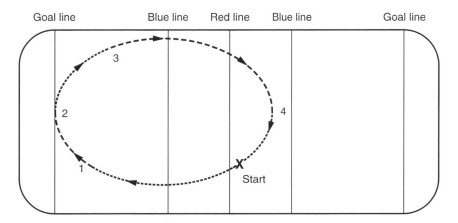

Figure 10.6 Agility exercise 2.

Exercise 3

Start from the goal line and follow the circular patterns shown in figure 10.7. The tightness of the pattern requires deep edges, strong knee bend, precise upper-body control, and balance. Skate rapidly.

Variations

1. Skate forward using the forward stride on the straightaways; skate one full time around the circles using forward crossovers. Alternate direction on each circle.
2. Skate backward using the backward stride on the straightaways; skate one full time around the circles using backward crossovers. Alternate direction on each circle.

3. Skate forward from the goal line. Turn from forward to backward at the near blue line and skate backward crossovers around the first circle. Skate one full time around the circle, counterclockwise. Turn from backward to forward at the center red line and skate forward crossovers around the second circle. Skate one full time around the circle, clockwise. Turn from forward to backward at the far blue line and skate straight backward to the far goal line. Alternate the exercise in order to practice forward and backward crossovers in both directions.

4. Skate forward and perform a pivot at the center red line (counterclockwise). Skate one full time around the circle using forward crossovers. On completing the first circle, again pivot at the red line (clockwise). Finish the second circle using forward crossovers. On reaching the far blue line, sprint forward to the far goal line.

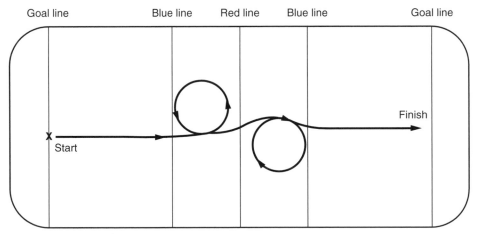

Figure 10.7 Agility exercise 3.

Exercise 4

Two players stand on the goal line, opposite each other and on opposite sides of the rink. Both players skate simultaneously. Neither player crosses the midline of the rink at any time. Refer to figure 10.8.

1. Skate forward from X to 1.
2. Turn backward at 1, chest facing outside the curve. Sprint backward to point 2.
3. Skate backward crossovers from 2 to 3. Turn forward at 3, chest facing inside the curve.
4. Skate forward crossovers between 3 and 4. Sprint forward between 4 and X.
5. Repeat, now starting backward. Turn forward at 1, chest facing outside the curve. Sprint forward to point 2. Use forward crossovers between 2 and 3. Turn backward at 3, chest facing inside the curve. Skate backward crossovers between 3 and 4. Sprint backward between 4 and X.

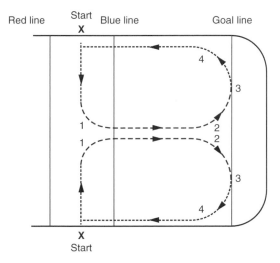

Figure 10.8 Agility exercise 4.

Exercise 5: Obstacle Course

Obstacle courses are fun and challenging. They should be modified according to age and ability levels. Refer to figure 10.9.

1. Sprint forward from X. Between 1 and 2 skate forward crossovers in and out of pylons.
2. At 3, jump over the stick; at 4, dive under the stick; at 5 jump over the stick again.
3. Between 6 and 7, perform 360-degree pivots. At 8, perform a lateral leap over the stick.
4. Between 9 and 10, execute forward crossovers in and out of pylons. Turn backward at 11.
5. Between 11 and 16, perform backward crossovers in and out of pylons. Turn forward at 16.
6. From 16 to X, sprint forward. Perform a hockey stop at the finish.
7. Repeat while carrying a puck.
8. Time your players when skating obstacle courses. As an incentive to perform properly, you may assess a penalty (.5 seconds) for each stick that is knocked over.

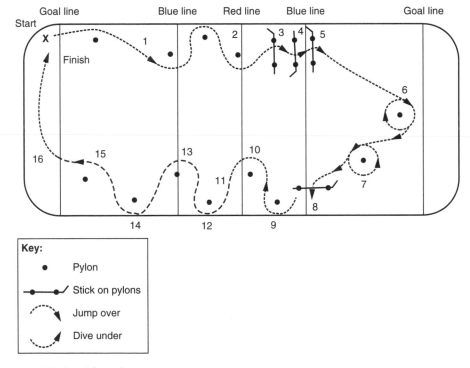

Figure 10.9 Obstacle course.

chapter 11

Training and Conditioning for Faster, More Powerful Skating

Hockey is a sport of intense physical and mental work. Games can go almost nonstop and can last up to four hours. Shifts range between 20 and 80 seconds and are filled with explosive bursts that are demanding and depleting. Top hockey players are precisely trained and finely conditioned athletes. Their muscles, honed for power, speed, explosive movement, and agility, are capable of working at peak performance even at the end of grueling shifts.

Throughout this book we stress the importance of correct, powerful, and rapid application of force. As shown, proper skating technique is extremely important for efficient speed and explosive acceleration. But conditioning is also important. The elements of conditioning for hockey skating are flexibility, endurance, strength, power, quickness, and agility. Players cannot skate powerfully or quickly if their muscles are poorly developed, and they cannot perform optimally in game situations if their cardiovascular systems are in less than prime condition.

Training and conditioning programs for hockey skating include all the above elements. Though the training regime for each element is different, all are interrelated and mutually dependent. For example, agility, which relies on flexibility, also relies on endurance. As fatigue sets in, agility decreases. Strength, power, speed, quickness, and skating technique also suffer as fatigue sets in. Awareness, visual acuity, and reflexes are similarly affected.

Only in recent years have coaches and sports scientists recognized that skating technique, as well as explosive speed, improves with proper training and conditioning. Before that it was generally accepted that "you can skate, or you can't skate" or "you're born to be fast or slow." Coaches and trainers now understand the value of training and conditioning in helping athletes reach their potential for speed.

There is no substitute for on-ice workouts. But a well-designed year-round training and conditioning program can help players skate faster than their current "fastest." Workouts should be designed to meet the needs of each individual and offer enough variety to maintain a high level of interest.

This chapter is an overview of the fundamentals of training and conditioning specific to hockey skating. For more in-depth knowledge, read and research some of the many sources on training and conditioning programs for hockey. You might also read up on such subjects as visualization, mental training, positive self-image, nutrition, hydration, fluid replacement, and proper rest. A few valuable publications are listed in the recommended reading section at the end of this book (page 224).

Although skating relies primarily on muscles of the hips, buttocks, and quadriceps, several other muscle groups of the lower and upper body are also used. For example, explosive starts require strong muscles of the feet, arches, ankles, calves, and hamstrings as well as quadriceps and buttocks. Full extension calls upon strong leg muscles, but also strong feet, ankles, and arches for the final push (toe flick). The outward/inward motions in skating call upon the adductors and abductors. To keep the back straight and under control, players use muscles of the back and chest. To torque, players must recruit muscles of the waist, chest, and back. Pushing powerfully also requires strong abdominal muscles. Arms and neck muscles must also be strong and flexible. In other words, hockey skating is very much a full-body workout.

Warm-Up and Cool-Down

As we know, hockey is a sport of explosive motions and sudden changes of direction. Muscles *cannot* be called upon to perform these movements until they are readied for work. The body must be gradually brought from a state of rest to a state of readiness for work in order to function optimally and reduce the likelihood of muscle and soft-tissue injuries associated with sudden movement.

It is easier to stretch muscles that are warm, so light warm-up activities such as slow skating, walking, or jogging, should be done for 5 to 10 minutes before stretching. After exercise there should be a cool-down phase. A light skate or slow walk for 5 to 10 minutes followed by 10 to 15 minutes of stretching gradually brings the body from a state of work to a state of rest. This is important to prevent tightening of and potential injuries to muscles.

Training for Flexibility

Improved flexibility brings several specific benefits to a hockey player's performance.

1. Flexibility allows for speedier movement of the engaged muscle groups. As muscles and joints become more flexible they give less resistance to movement. This allows them to apply force more rapidly and in a greater range of motion. As the speed of applied force increases, power also increases.

2. As flexibility increases, so does agility. Flexible muscles and joints can work more efficiently through their full range of motion.

3. Flexibility delays the onset of fatigue. Increased flexibility reduces resistance as the muscles and joints move through their full range of motion. The amount of energy required is also reduced, so the activity can be prolonged.

4. As flexibility increases the likelihood of muscle injury is decreased. Players who are flexible are generally less prone to injuries.

Flexibility is developed through proper and consistent stretching. It increases if athletes adhere to an *ongoing* stretching program. Flexibility should be valued as highly as technique and strength training.

Stretching serves three functions—first, to prepare the body for work; second, to develop body flexibility; and third, to cool down muscles after heavy exercise. Since ice time during the playing season is generally limited, off-ice stretching is advisable unless the stretching exercises are being used to also work on balance. During the off-season all players should engage in daily stretching sessions.

Since skating utilizes muscles of both the lower and upper body, stretching exercises for both are necessary. Start each stretch slowly and gently, and gradually try to increase the range of motion of each muscle group. Stretch for a minimum of 10 minutes before each workout and 10 to 15 minutes after each workout. Dancers begin each workout by stretching at a bar for about 30 minutes before jumping and spinning on the floor. Keep this in mind when planning your stretching program.

Warm muscles are easier to stretch than cold muscles. Therefore some light warm-up activities should precede each stretching routine. Stretch again after each workout. This may help to prevent the injuries caused by sudden tightening of muscles when exercise ends too abruptly.

Stretching Procedure

Perform each stretch in a slow, sustained manner to the point where you feel light tension (but not pain) in the stretched muscles. Hold this position for about 20 to 30 seconds. Relax and ease off for about 10 seconds. Then increase the stretch to a point of greater tension. Hold this position for another 20 to 30 seconds. Do not bounce, as this may cause injuries.

Nonmoving stretches should be done away from the ice whenever possible so as to preserve precious ice time for skating-related exercises.

For young people or people who are very flexible, stretching exercises should be quite safe. Those getting back into shape after an injury or a period of inactivity should be careful not to lock (hyperextend) joints or to put undue stress on the back, hips, neck, and knees.

Key areas to consider when stretching:

- Abdominals
- Abductors
- Achilles tendons
- Adductors
- Ankles
- Arms
- Back
- Calves
- Feet
- Gluteals
- Hamstrings
- Hips
- Neck
- Shoulders
- Quadriceps
- Waist
- Wrists

Change stretches periodically to make the stretching routine interesting and fun. Refer to *Complete Conditioning for Ice Hockey* by Peter Twist or *Sports Stretch* (3rd edition) by Michael J. Alter for more information on stretching.

Training for Endurance

Because of its intensity and duration, hockey requires that players possess *exceptional* endurance. Hockey combines explosive speed with powerful body checking, forceful maneuvering, and fighting for the puck. Sometimes bursts of speed are short and intense with moments of slower skating or coasting in between. At other times players skate without relief for entire shifts. Players must be conditioned so that they can recover from these intense work periods during each brief rest period on the bench. Whatever the game situation, players must have sufficient energy reserves to give their all, even toward the end of a long and exhausting game.

The body has two types of energy sources, each yielding a different form of endurance. We will refer to these forms of endurance as wind (aerobic) and explosive (anaerobic) endurance.

Aerobic Endurance

The aerobic system is the body's most efficient, and therefore the most important, source of energy. Aerobic endurance relies on the oxygen (aerobic) system to produce energy and the muscle cells to use that energy. Aerobic fitness is the base for all training and conditioning. Strength, power, and speed are impossible unless the athlete has established a strong foundation of aerobic endurance.

When we breathe we take in oxygen, which the heart, lungs, and blood vessels transport to all parts of the body. Oxygen combines with the nutrients in the cells to produce energy for work. To improve the aerobic system the heart must be conditioned to pump more blood per beat. As the heart and circulatory system become more efficient, athletes can work harder and longer with less stress before becoming fatigued, and can recover more quickly to perform at top efficiency.

Aerobic training involves stressing the oxygen system by forcing the heart to beat at a higher rate than normal. This improves its ability to deliver oxygen to the muscles for energy and for the body to recover more quickly from intense work.

There are two types of aerobic workouts—*continuous* and *interval.* Continuous aerobic workouts are done at submaximal speeds and are designed to bring the heartbeat to 75 to 80 percent of its maximum rate during each workout of 30 to 60 minutes, three to four times a week. The heart rate during work periods is brought to 160 to 180 beats per minute. (The exact number of beats per minute depends on age—the older the athlete, the lower the number of beats per minute.)

Interval training alternates specific periods of work with specific periods of rest. Work–rest ratios vary according to the purpose of the specific workout (endurance, strength, power, or quickness) as well as the time of year. Workouts become more intense as the hockey season progresses. Interval workouts can be conducted on dry land as well as on the ice.

Interval aerobic workouts use sets of higher-intensity work (two to three minutes' duration) to bring the heart rate to within five beats of its maximum rate. This is followed by two to three minutes of rest (1:1 work–rest ratio). Interval training builds the aerobic supply and increases the muscles' ability to extract oxygen from the blood.

With aerobic training, the heart, lungs, and blood vessels adapt to the greater demands and their capacity to transport oxygen is increased. The muscles also adapt and their ability to utilize energy improves.

Exercises for Improving Aerobic Endurance

Since aerobic endurance workouts are performed at submaximal speeds, it is recommended that they be done mostly off-ice so that the submaximal speeds do not negatively affect quickness on the ice. Many sports improve aerobic endurance. Running (distance and interval), bicycling, dancing, hiking (hills), rock climbing, aerobic dance, swimming, handball, racket sports, basketball, soccer, gymnastics, and in-line skating are just a few.

Interval workouts bring about fatigue. Because fatigue negatively affects skating technique, skating drills in which the top priority is endurance are not recommended for young and developing skaters. Fatigue encourages bad skating habits that we don't want young players to develop.

The following on-ice drills are effective for improving aerobic endurance. They can also be practiced on in-line skates. Keep in mind that the submaximal leg speeds of endurance workouts are not the leg speeds needed for hockey. It is important to alternate endurance activities with quickness activities (see "Training for Quickness," page 211).

On-Ice Endurance Exercises

1. Skate continuous laps at half speed for 10 minutes. Skate easily and coast (rest period) for 5 minutes. Repeat. Do this for 20 to 30 minutes.

2. Do the same, skating at half speed for 20 minutes and skating easily for 10 minutes.

3. Skate laps around the rink alternately skating slowly, moderately (three-quarters speed), and short sprints (between blue lines), for 15 to 20 minutes.

4. Skate 15 laps around the rink using only four strides for the length of the ice. Skate at three-quarters speed around the corners. Skate easily and coast for 5 minutes. Do this for 20 to 30 minutes.

5. Combine these exercises or create others similar in format. Perform them skating backward as well and alternate the direction in which you skate around the rink to practice crossovers in both directions.

In-Line Skating

In-line skates have wheels that simulate the ice skate blade, but because the wheels do not grip the ground as well as edges grip the ice some ice skating maneuvers are difficult to do. For example, in-line wheels cannot be leaned as extremely as ice skates, so turns have a wider curve. Additionally, it is difficult to make wheels slide sideways along the ground the way skate blades slide on the ice, so stopping is more difficult. However, the principles of edges still apply, and the use of leg drive and body weight are very similar (figure 11.1).

Figure 11.1 In-line skating can be great off-ice exercise endurance training.

In-line skating can be effectively used for endurance training while incorporating skating-specific muscles in skating-specific motions. It is important to note that the weight of in-line skates may encourage leg speeds that are too slow for ice hockey. They are therefore not recommended for quickness training. Wear full protective equipment whenever skating on in-line skates. Falls on hard pavement hurt and can cause serious injuries!

Anaerobic Endurance

For sudden, intense bursts of power, the oxygen system alone is insufficient to fulfill the energy demands of the body. In these situations, additional energy is supplied by the muscle cells themselves. Nutrients within the cells (stored glycogen) are converted into energy (in the form of sugar) for work in the absence of oxygen. In this *anaerobic* process of energy production, waste products in the form of lactic acid are given off and accumulate in the muscle cells.

The accumulation of lactic acid in the cells causes rapid fatigue and a decrease in coordination, speed, balance, and overall skill. Although the anaerobic energy system is critical to explosive movement, it is not nearly as efficient as the aerobic system in producing large quantities of energy.

Anaerobic training improves the efficiency of the cellular energy system—its ability to convert stored glycogen into sugar for energy and to remove waste products from the muscle cells. The more efficient the cellular energy system, the more quickly it can transport waste products back into the bloodstream, thereby reducing the concentration of lactic acid within the cells.

Anaerobic training and conditioning allows players to perform with greater accumulations of waste products in the muscle cells before succumbing to fatigue. They are better prepared to skate explosively for an entire shift and recover completely during brief rest periods on the bench.

Anaerobic training consists of short bursts of intense activity and slightly longer intense activity. In both cases the activity must be performed at 100 percent effort. The activity is then followed by a rest period of two to three times the duration of the activity, so the body can transfer waste products (lactic acid) from the cells into the bloodstream. Full recovery is essential for optimum performance.

While training the anaerobic system, incorporate exercises that use skating-specific motions and skating-specific muscle groups. Dry land activities such as in-line skating and slideboard training develop anaerobic endurance while utilizing the skating motion and using muscle groups in skating-specific ways.

The slideboard (figure 11.2) was made famous as a training device by Olympic speed skating champion Eric Heiden. It is an excellent device for power training (use short work intervals such as 20 seconds:60 seconds) as well as endurance training (use longer work intervals such as 40 seconds:80 seconds). It is also excellent for practicing the motions of the forward skating stride (technique development). It can be easily built.

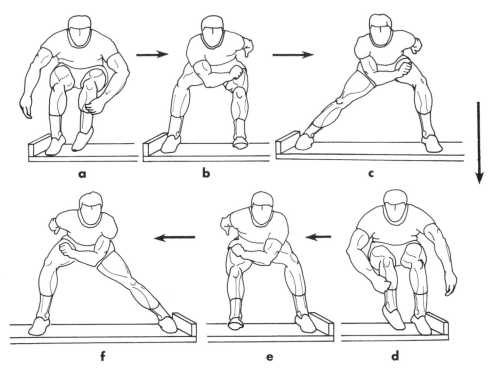

Figure 11.2 Heiden slideboard: Note the similarity to the forward skating stride.

Exercises for Improving Anaerobic Endurance

Off-Ice Exercises

Sprint for 50 meters and then walk or jog slowly to rest. Rest two to three times as long as it took to sprint. Do the same for 100, 200, 300, and 400 meters as well as distances in-between.

Interval training on a bicycle and hiking (especially on hills) are effective anaerobic workouts.

On-Ice Exercises

Train with short, explosive sprints of 5 to 15 seconds followed by slow skating. Also do longer sprints of up to 45 seconds followed by a rest period long enough to allow for total recovery. Use a work–rest ratio of 1:2 (sometimes a ratio of 1:3 is called for). Also, alternate skating intervals as follows:

100 percent effort for 15 seconds, easily for 45 seconds; 100 percent effort for 30 seconds, easily for 90 seconds; 100 percent effort for 45 seconds, easily for 90 seconds; 75 percent effort for 45 seconds, easily for 90 seconds; and 100 percent effort for 15 seconds, easily for 45 seconds.

Guidelines for On-Ice Endurance Training Intervals

When training for *aerobic* endurance, high-level players generally use intervals with a work–rest ratio of 1:1—skating at three-quarters speed for 60 seconds, then skating slowly (resting) for 60 seconds.

When training for *anaerobic* endurance, they skate with maximum effort, using a work–rest ratio of 1:2—skating all-out for 40 seconds, resting for 80 seconds. When performing explosive stops and starts, a work–rest ratio of 1:3 is appropriate—skating at maximum effort for 30 seconds, resting for 90 seconds.

The top priority on ice for young (under the age of 15) and learning skaters is technique, not endurance. On-ice drills specifically designed for anaerobic endurance are counterproductive. As fatigue sets in, these players will necessarily resort to poor skating techniques, and the bad habits developed under these circumstances may be difficult to change. Use light aerobic interval training on the ice and avoid fatigue.

Endurance for young players can be developed by many off-ice activities, some of which have been previously mentioned. On-ice endurance for young players may be developed by the following:

1. The sum of all on-ice practice drills (60- to 90-minute sessions).
2. On-ice sprints at practice tempo. Keep work periods short enough that fatigue does not destroy skating technique or skill development.

Some endurance workouts should be aerobic, to build the all-important aerobic base; others should be anaerobic. When planning an endurance program, keep in mind that off-ice activities do not interfere with skating skill. Therefore, these activities offer the most productive opportunity for endurance training.

Training for Strength

Developing strength for its own sake is not an appropriate goal for hockey players. Their need for strength lies in the ability to apply that strength explosively. When strength is applied explosively, power results. Power combined with rapid leg motion results in speed. Strength is, of course, a critical component of power and speed, as well as explosive acceleration and BAM, so it must be developed.

I teach so many adolescent players who have gone through recent growth spurts; their muscle strength has not caught up with their bone length. They look strong but skate weakly. They can't seem to bend their knees enough, push hard or quickly enough, or skate with agility or explosiveness. These players are at the in-between stage: too young to engage in heavy strength-training programs, and old enough to know this soon will be a necessity.

What many adolescent players don't know is that it's not just their upper bodies they must develop—not to look good in the bathing suit, but to strengthen the skating muscles (legs). All great skaters have strong quads and glutes. Regular strength workouts pay off in the long run.

Strong, flexible muscles are essential not only for power and speed, but also for minimizing injury to soft tissues and joints. Players must strengthen all the muscle groups used in hockey—those of the lower and upper body used for explosive skating, as well as those of the upper body used for shooting, checking, and withstanding body blows.

Strength training is the process of building muscle mass and recruiting more of the existing muscle fibers for work. Muscle mass can be gained from a variety of workouts that involve working against heavy resistance at various speeds (for example, weightlifting at slow speeds). Muscle fiber recruitment is improved by lifting at specific speeds.

Strength training requires that the muscles to be strengthened be progressively overloaded. Adhering to the *overload principle* is critical; muscles, after being repeatedly forced to work beyond their present capability, eventually adapt to the new work level and perform more effectively. At this point they must be overloaded again to develop an even greater capability for work. As long as the overload principle is followed, a variety of training methods can be used to achieve the same results. All require the muscles to work against resistance. Calisthenics, isometric training, partner resistance, and weight training are acceptable methods of increasing strength.

Note: Players under the age of 16 should not engage in programs that rely on working against *heavy* resistance or weights.

Overloading is achieved in a number of ways: increasing the load to be moved (resistance or weight); increasing the length of each training session, the number of training sessions, or the number of repetitions and or/ the number of sets per exercise. Strength training takes place mostly off ice.

The muscles of the lower body to be strengthened for skating are those of the hips, gluteals, adductors (groin), abductors (outer thighs), quadriceps, hamstrings, calves, and feet and ankles. The muscles of the upper body to be strengthened are those of the abdominals, back, chest, shoulders, arms, and neck. Keep in mind that the muscles of the upper body are used for skating as well as for shooting, checking, etc. For example, the back is used to control excessive upper-body movement (balance and stability). The chest and arms are used to create correct and powerful arm swing. The abdominals assist in pushing. With all strength training, it is important to train the muscles on both sides of the joint to maintain stability.

Calisthenics

Calisthenic exercises use one's own body weight as the resistance to be moved. Exercises include pushups, situps, leg lifts, trunk raises, side and hip raises, wall squats, chinning, and many others. Young players can do light calisthenics.

Calisthenics should be done off the ice to preserve valuable ice time. These workouts are valuable, necessary, even enjoyable, and they produce positive results. They should be an integral part of every training regimen and should not be used to punish.

Isometric Training

This type of training involves balanced and opposing equal forces of two or more complementary muscle groups. Use arms to oppose legs, use arms and legs to oppose the central torso, use a given muscle group to oppose a fixed surface, use a partner to resist movement of legs or arms, or just power-flex one group of muscles (such as the abdominals) until sufficient overload is achieved. Isometrics are especially useful when expensive weight-training equipment is not readily available. They can be done by young players.

Here is a sample isometric exercise: Lie on the floor, legs stretched in front of you, one on either side of a straight-legged chair. Press your legs inward against the chair. This simple exercise strengthens the adductor (groin) muscles. You can also pair up with a partner to perform isometric exercises.

Resistance Exercises

There are many devices that can be used to fulfill the overload principle by creating resistance when walking, running, or skating. Some of these devices include weight belts, weight vests (or weighted backpacks), parachutes (speed chutes), leashes, and bungee cords.

Partner Resistance on the Ice

This type of resistance makes use of the overload principle by moving (skating) while pulling against a partner who is resisting the movement. Many skating moves can be practiced, some even by young players, against partner resistance, as long as the partner is of similar size and weight.

Weight Training

Muscles are overloaded by the use of progressively heavier weights (dumbbells, barbells, machines, and such). Begin training programs with light weights. Gradually increase the weight to be moved. Vary the weight-training routine from session to session in order to work different muscle groups. Weight training for strength development ultimately requires heavy loads. Learn to lift correctly to avoid injury. Weight-training programs should be designed for each individual and supervised by knowledgeable instructors.

Remember, strength-training exercises tighten muscles. Warm up, stretch, and cool down gradually before and after each strength-training session.

Pavel Bure exhibits the benefits of good training and conditioning with his superb knee bend, outside edge, balance, and upper body position for crossovers with his chest facing into the curve.

Training for Power

Power results when strength is applied explosively. Power accompanied by rapid leg motion results in speed. One way to conceptualize the expression of power is to compare muscles to the pistons in an automobile engine. The power stroke of an engine occurs when the compressed fuel-air mixture is exploded by a spark; the force of the explosion drives the piston and thus powers the automobile. Leg strength is a necessary component of speed, but only if applied explosively (powerfully and rapidly) and correctly. Efficient and effective speed result when power and quickness are utilized in the correct skating motion. Watch Jaromir Jagr skate and you will see a demonstration of power converted into speed.

Power training, like strength training, requires that *specific* muscle groups be progressively overloaded, but at the same time the athlete must increase the speed of motion (explosiveness) while working against resistance. *Power skating* requires that the muscles specific to skating work explosively in the same range of motion as in skating and at the same speed as (or even faster than) required by the sport of hockey.

Power-training workouts should be structured so that the athlete progressively increases the number of repetitions of each set of exercises while decreasing the time needed to work through each set. It is important to continue working at speed even when fatigued, the purpose being to get beyond that threshold of fatigue and reach a new tolerance. (Note, however, that after a certain point, increasing the number of sets or repetitions in each set improves endurance but not power.)

A good general rule for using weights for power training is to lift (or push or pull) 50 to 60 percent of *your* maximum weight capability for five sets of each exercise, with five repetitions in each set. Training with *maximum* loads increases strength, but because the speed is necessarily slow, power cannot be maximized. Training with loads too light produces very fast movement but the force is too low to develop power.

Each lift should be done with as much speed as possible. Attempt to accelerate to the *end* of the range of motion on every lift. Acceleration and intensity are key factors. Doing squat jumps while wearing a weighted vest or belt exemplifies the effort to accelerate throughout the full range of motion. Work–rest ratios of power workouts must include a long enough rest period between sets or exercises so that each set can be performed explosively and with speed (full recovery time). If speed is slow, power is low.

Power training causes fatigue. Complete recovery is essential so that the system can rest, rebuild, and adapt to a new level of work capability and fatigue tolerance. Muscle rebuilding after intense power workouts takes up to 48 hours, so power-training workouts should be scheduled at least two days apart. Other types of workouts can be done in-between.

Power-Training Workouts

As with endurance training, most (but not all) power training should take place off-ice so as not to interfere with quality skating. As with strength training, power training that relies on relatively heavy resistance is not recommended for skaters under 15 years of age.

Off-Ice Workouts

Running uphill, interval running, slideboards, bicycling (uphill), interval workouts on a stationary bike, calisthenics, plyometric exercises (movements that involve a recoil–spring principle), and partner resistance—all while wearing some weighted device at submaximal resistance—are all methods of power training on dry land. In-line skating can also be used for power training, When using in-line skates for power training, skate uphill wearing a submaximal resistance device. Coast down if the hill is slight, and walk down if the hill is very steep. Power training on in-line skates is especially useful because the movements are specific to and in the range of motion of ice skating, so the skater can (until fatigue sets in) also practice skating technique.

On-Ice Workouts

Some on-ice power training is essential. Skating explosively against resistance is an essential aspect of power training on-ice. Wearing a weight vest or weight belt, skating against partner resistance, or doing plyometric skating drills are all excellent means of accomplishing this.

Note: Muscles should not be overloaded too much, because the fatigued skater will resort to poor skating techniques. Poor skating habits, often difficult to correct, may result.

Interval training is effective in developing powerful leg drive. It is also important to move the legs rapidly. Use a work–rest ratio of 1:5. For example, skate for 10 seconds, rest for 50 seconds; skate for 20 seconds, rest for 100 seconds. Wear weighted vests or belts with 50 to 60 percent of the maximum weight moved in strength training (only for players 16 years or older).

Plyometrics

One of the most effective means of training for power is *plyometrics* (recoil bounding). Plyometrics links strength and sprint speed. Plyometric exercises involve a quick recoil preceding an explosive spring. They involve a coil–uncoil, stretch–contract action of the muscles. Examples are bounding, hopping, broad jumping, squat jumps, leaping (forward and backward, or laterally) over an obstacle, or jumping up stairs, all of which require great spring and agility.

Plyometric training is hard on the joints. It is not recommended for those with medical conditions that limit joint function. Remember, it is important to establish flexibility and strength around the joints before participating in strenuous plyometric workouts.

Plyometric training works as follows:

1. Recoiling acts as a wind-up. The muscles, during the recoil, are stretched. Stretched muscles and tissues store energy like a rubber band. That stored energy becomes available for use upon muscle contraction.

2. When muscles are stretched quickly they contract actively in a reflex interaction with nerves. This quick stretch–contract interactive pattern makes it possible to recruit muscle fibers in a more powerful manner.

Plyometric Exercises

All plyometric exercises involve a deep knee bend, a spring into the air, then another deep knee bend upon landing.

Off-Ice Exercises

There are hundreds of plyometric exercises that are excellent for the skating muscles. Most are done off the ice, but there are many that can be done on the ice as well. Following are just a few examples of plyometric exercises.

Step-Up, Step-Down

Step up onto a low bench (about 15 to 18 inches high) with your right foot and then with your left foot, so that both feet are on the bench. Then step back down with your right foot, then your left foot, so that both feet are on the floor. Keep repeating rapidly. Do the same exercise stepping up with your left foot and down with your right foot.

Standing Broad Jumps

Standing broad jumps are one of the most effective plyometric maneuvers for skating; they are also an excellent means of practicing front starts on dry land.

Perform continuous standing broad jumps on flat ground and on slight inclines. Do 5 to 30 in a row. Concentrate on the coil–spring principle and on achieving as much forward distance as possible (see figure 11.3, a-c).

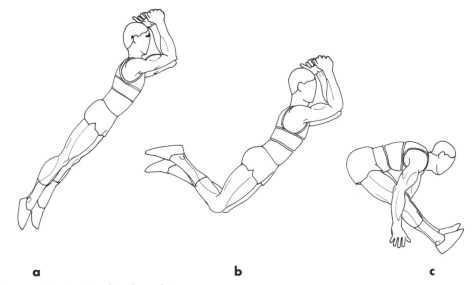

a   b   c

Figure 11.3 Standing broad jumps.

Jumps and Hops

See chapter 2 for instructions for these exercises. These can be done on dry land or on ice.

On-Ice Exercises

Inside Edge Jumps

Set up an imaginary axis, or line, along the length of the ice and approximately 20 feet from the sideboards on your right. Skate forward, then glide on the RFI, aiming the glide directly away from the axis. Maintain a strong edge and knee bend during the glide. Skate a counterclockwise semicircle.

When you have curved a full 180 degrees, jump from the right skate as high off the ice as possible and land on the LFI. Land on a deep inside edge with strong knee bend of the left leg. Maintaining the edge and knee bend, glide on the LFI, aiming the glide directly away from the axis and skate a clockwise semicircle.

When you have curved a full 180 degrees, jump from the left skate as high off the ice as possible. Land on a deep RFI with a strong knee bend of the right leg. You have completed one cycle. Repeat this cycle until you have completed one length of the ice.

Remember: To balance, keep your back straight with your eyes and head up. Keep the free skate off the ice and close to the gliding skate during each jump (figure 11.4).

Variations

1. Perform Inside Edge Jumps, but skate on, jump from, and land on *outside* edges.
2. Perform the jumps skating backward.

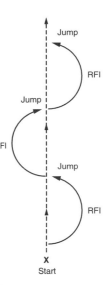

Figure 11.4 Inside edge jumps.

S Jumps

Refer to the S-Cuts exercise, chapter 6, page 93.

Just like the S-Cuts exercise, this is performed on one skate at a time. When changing from outside edge (RFO) to inside edge (RFI) or inside edge (RFI) to outside edge (RFO), jump off the ice to change the edge.

Jump as high off the ice as possible and land on a deep edge with a strong knee bend on the landing leg. Keep the free skate off the ice and hold it close to the gliding skate during each jump. See how many S-cuts you can make before putting the free skate on the ice. Keep back straight, eyes and head up. Repeat the exercise skating on the left skate. Then perform the exercise skating backward on each skate.

Training for Quickness

Quickness means fast feet, rapid leg motion. It refers to a player's ability to accelerate between point A and point B, either from a dead stop or from slow to fast. It is one of the most important qualities a hockey player can possess, for it vitally influences the ability to rev up! It often determines who gets to the puck first or who gets a breakaway opportunity.

Quickness is enhanced by a combination of factors, including proper skating technique, explosive power, and rapid leg motion. Quickness training involves improving leg speed while still moving the legs through their full range of motion. Until recently it was assumed that quickness is an innate quality. Now we know that quickness can be improved with proper training.

The younger a player begins training for quickness, the greater the potential for development. As players get older they must continue to train for quickness or this quality will diminish, just as flexibility, strength, power, and endurance diminish if they are not continuously trained.

Quickness training requires skating at top speed in all-out, explosive workouts. The bursts are intense and of short duration. Resistance is not used. Since quickness training forces players into an anaerobic state, long rest periods that allow for full recovery from fatigue are essential for the athlete to perform each repetition optimally.

The principles for achieving explosive acceleration and sprint speed in skating are virtually identical to those in running. The technical differences between the two lie in the differences in the surfaces pushed against; these require that the pushes be executed differently. Figure 11.5, a-b shows the similarities between explosive skating starts and explosive running starts.

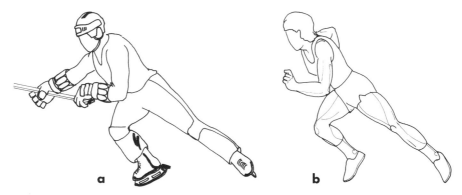

Figure 11.5   Explosive starts: skating and running.

Quickness-Training Workouts

The purpose of quickness-training workouts is to develop fast feet and sprint speed. Workouts must be done at top speed at all times. They are nontechnical in nature. Since the intensity of quickness training can destroy skating technique, it is advantageous to do quickness workouts on dry land. These workouts require total concentration and maximum effort. Players must be fresh and completely warmed up. Never do quickness workouts when fatigued or following strength or power workouts.

Since workouts involve no resistance, they can be performed daily with alternating workout intensities. Perform light workouts one day and heavy workouts the next. Movement must be fast paced. Slow movement trains slowness.

Quickness training does not focus on conditioning although improved conditioning is a by-product.

Work intervals should be short, rest intervals long. A work–rest ratio of 1:5 or 1:10 allows for total recovery. This is necessary for each repetition to be performed with full intensity and optimum effort. For example, sprint at maximum speed and effort for 10 seconds, rest for 50 seconds; sprint for 5 seconds, rest for 40 seconds; sprint for 8 seconds, rest for 40 to 80 seconds. The same applies for skating sprints.

Off-Ice Workouts

Sprint biking, sprint running (such as the 30-meter dash), and slight downhill sprints are some of the means of quickness training on dry land. Because of their weight, in-line skates are not recommended for quickness training.

Workouts for developing overall speed include running a 30-meter dash, a 60-meter dash, or a 100-meter dash. Leave enough time between sprints for complete recovery (work–rest ratio of 1:5).

Explosive starts can be practiced on a track, on sand, or on grass. Explosive acceleration on the first five steps is of primary importance. To work on starts, run 20-meter sprints. Run from a standstill. Start both forward and sideways. Standing broad jumps (figure 11.3) help develop the "falling" feeling experienced in explosive starts. Racing dives in a pool simulate the same feeling.

Variations of quickness training on dry land are many:

- Sprint 20 meters, cut sharply to the side, sprint again, cut sharply to the other side.
- Incorporate crossovers, lateral leaps, sprints up and down slight inclines, and/or running backward. Do different combinations of these moves at top, even out-of-control, speeds.
- Swing a bat and run to first base. This simulates the lateral weight shift and outward-falling feeling necessary for explosive crossover (side) starts.

Another aspect of quickness is BAM: balance, agility, and maneuverability. Coordination and flexibility exercises such as tumbling, rolling, jumping, hopping, juggling, gymnastic moves, dribbling balls with the feet, running obstacle courses, performing moves with no previous knowledge of the move (all while moving fast), are good ways to improve BAM.

Remember: Quality, intensity, and top speed are essential for quickness workouts. When you're tired and quality is suffering or when you're not accomplishing anything, switch to another kind of workout. If muscles are sore, delay quickness work until the soreness is gone.

On-Ice Workouts

The goal on ice is to develop the fastest possible leg rhythm while still moving the legs correctly, powerfully, and through their full range of motion. Since skill and quickness on ice are developed while skating, most on-ice skating drills should be geared toward skill and speed development rather than endurance development. Once correct skating techniques are established, on-ice sprint intervals may be the most important aspect of a player's training program. With or without the puck, the point is to perform everything at *top speed.* In game situations and even in practices, players rarely skate as fast as they would if they were being timed. Players slow down to carry the puck, receive passes, or wait for the play. In practices they inadvertently slow down, fearing a fall or loss of the puck in front of their coach or teammates.

The neuromuscular system can be likened to a computer: It records for future performance everything we do, whether fast or slow, correct or incorrect. If you practice skating technique only at slow speeds, the neuromuscular system will pass that information on and you will learn to skate correctly but slowly. You *must* learn to skate correctly, then to skate correctly *fast* (Blatherwick, 1986).

Training to become a great hockey skater is a long and methodical process. First learn to execute correctly (technique training); then correctly and powerfully; then correctly, powerfully, and quickly; then, correctly, powerfully, and quickly with the puck; finally, correctly, powerfully, and quickly with the puck, in game situations and under lots of pressure.

Over-Speed Training

Quickness on the ice requires you to perform skating maneuvers at ever-increasing speeds. At a certain point, it is necessary to practice them at *out-of-control* speeds. This training is nontechnical in nature. It is better to fall and/or lose the puck during over-speed workouts than to slow down just to avoid mistakes or losing control. In fact, players should push themselves to speeds that *cause* mistakes. It's called "getting out of your comfort zone."

Out-of-control skating maneuvers must be repeated again and again until players become comfortable at the *new* speed. Then they must go beyond that speed, to a new out-of-control speed, again making mistakes as they practice, until they are comfortable at that new level of speed. When combined with slower drills to learn and improve technique, these sprints increase the ability to perform difficult maneuvers at top speed while *in control.* Strive for progressively greater speed, increased quickness, more agility, and the three Cs—*control, composure,* and *comfort* (Wenger, 1986). Players who achieve the three Cs have attained the ability to perform intricate maneuvers at top speed in game situations.

The following sprint exercises described for over-speed training on dry land can also be done on ice. Keep the on-ice sprints short (20 to 100 yards or meters), leaving time for full recovery between repetitions. Other dry land exercises can be used on ice as well: tumbling, jumping, hopping, juggling, dribbling pucks with the feet, skating obstacle courses, and performing a variety of skating moves with no previous knowledge of the moves. All moves must be performed while skating *fast*.

Mental Quickness

Another aspect of quickness training is mental quickness, or mental preparedness. The ability to anticipate, make quick decisions, and respond instantly to changing conditions can be learned and enhanced by awareness training. Players who learn to know where others are and what others are doing while they themselves are performing intricate maneuvers at great speed are the ones who anticipate, read plays, react, and move quickly in games. Mental quickness was one of Wayne Gretzky's greatest attributes.

Awareness and Visual Acuity

Train yourself to be aware of teammates and opponents as much of the time as possible. This awareness can be increased considerably by developing peripheral vision. Practice by focusing on a point directly in front of you. Concentrate on seeing out of the corners of your eyes. Mentally list everything you see. Practice determining color and spotting movement at the corners of your vision. Have someone hold up various colored objects off to one side and then the other. Keep your eyes focused straight ahead as your partner brings the objects slowly into your field of vision from behind you and off to the sides. Call out "now" followed by the color as soon as you can see the movement. With practice you can more quickly spot pucks, sticks, and players, and also determine the colors of jerseys. There are many techniques for training the eyes to move quickly. This type of training is essential for hockey players, and especially important for goalies.

Dry Land Training for Skating Technique

With ice time as precious as it is, and with the overwhelming amount of skill work that must be covered in limited practice sessions, it is advantageous to use dry land training to develop and practice correct skating movements.

Dry land skating, used for technique training, offers several advantages:

1. Skaters can practice the exact motions and body positions of the skating strides (forward, backward, crossovers, starts, and so on) in a slow, exaggerated manner.

2. Coaches can give instruction, have discussions, and answer questions away from the ice, freeing ice time for implementing and practicing skating moves.

3. Already discussed are the benefits of slideboards and in-line skates to simulate skating strides and practice skating technique off the ice. The activities are different but the motions and muscles are similar. (Figure 11.2 illustrates the use of a slideboard.)

When used to develop and practice correct skating techniques, dry land training should initially be conducted at low levels of speed and resistance so players can Feel, Act, See, and Think (FAST) about executing each segment of the skating move. In the learning stages, each movement should be exaggerated, and each stride and position executed as perfectly as possible. Technique and fitness should *not* be trained together—there is a time to concentrate on developing correct technique just as there is a time to concentrate on conditioning.

Remember: Fatigue destroys technique! As the correct motions and body positions become ingrained, the speed of execution should be gradually increased until each skating maneuver can be performed correctly at top speed.

Some dry land exercises that can be used to practice skating technique are shown in figures 11.6 through 11.10. When performing dry land skating exercises, apply the principles of body weight, knee bend, and the push–recovery sequence of the specific skating stride being practiced.

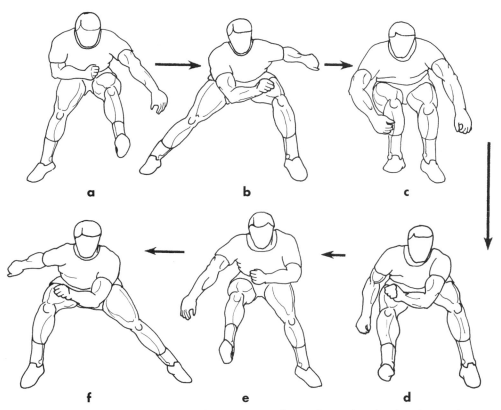

Figure 11.6 Lateral skating: Make skating motions from side to side rather than forward; note knee bend of support leg.

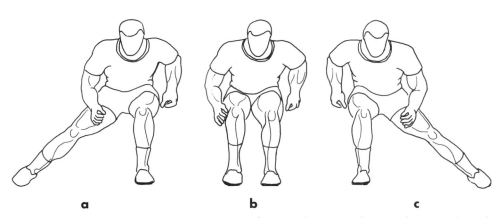

Figure 11.7 Side steps: Push to side; return feet together, using the same leg to push each time; maintain deep knee bend as the leg returns.

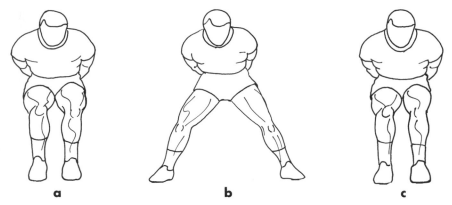

Figure 11.8 In-and-out jumps: Jump out in split-like position; return legs under body, maintaining knee bend as legs return.

Figure 11.9 Crossovers: Practice crossover/crossunder moves; note full extension of pushing leg under the body.

Figure 11.10 Sprint starts: Practice sprint starts on a track, starting both from a frontal and side position.

Maintaining the Level of Conditioning

When involved in a heavy schedule of competition, it is impossible to continue a rigid conditioning program. To hold the training effect at a high level but to avoid the fatigue that accompanies heavy training during these times, hockey players should go on a maintenance program. Decrease the duration of training sessions but keep the intensity high. Also, decrease the number of workouts to once or twice a week or as scheduling allows.

At all times it is important to get enough rest, follow a quality diet, and drink *lots* of water before, during, and after skating, playing, and working out.

Other Sports

Hockey is hard and intense work—it is very important to relax and take a break once in a while. During the off-season, other sports provide variety and are excellent supplements to hockey-specific training. Sports that involve running, such as basketball, soccer, track, and racket sports, use the leg muscles in different motions than skating but develop overall coordination, strength, quickness, agility, and endurance. Sports such as rowing, paddling, swimming, and wrestling develop and improve upper-body strength and power. Jumping rope (on a cushioned surface) is great for developing balance and quickness. Dancing and lateral or backward running are excellent for improving balance, coordination, and agility. Cycling, in-line skating (especially on hills), and walking or running on an inclined track are excellent workouts for the quadriceps.

Points to Remember

- Use proper warm-up and cool-down activities.
- Stretch conscientiously before and after workouts.
- Use a combination of on-ice and dry-land training methods to improve skating.
- Overload for strength and power.
- Underload for quickness and agility.
- Vary work–rest ratios and intensities in interval work to develop aerobic and anaerobic endurance.
- On the ice, combine correct skating technique with power, quickness, and agility—the formula for speed.
- On-ice sprint intervals are essential for developing the ability to apply power in a rapid skating motion.

- Quality skating drills combining speed work with technique work are the most important ingredients of training to be a great hockey skater.
- Repetition guarantees that learning will be permanent. But only *correct* repetition guarantees that learning will be *correct* and *permanent*. Only perfect practice makes perfect, so practice perfectly.

glossary

Abductor muscles—The muscles of the outer thigh, used to push the leg away from the center of the body.

Adductor muscles—The muscles of the inner thigh and groin, used to draw the leg inward toward the center of the body.

Aerobic—In the presence of oxygen.

Anaerobic—In the absence of oxygen.

Ball of the foot—The metatarsal area of the foot, immediately behind the toes.

Center of gravity—That segment or part of the body under which the feet must be situated in order to maintain balance or generate power.

Centrifugal force—The force that impels a body outward from the center of rotation.

Centripetal force—The force that impels a body inward toward the center of rotation.

Counter—The reinforced arch support of the skates.

Crossover—The two-step sequence used to maneuver and gain speed on a curve. The inside skate glides on the outside edge of the blade as the outside leg thrusts from the inside edge. After the thrust, the outside skate crosses over in front of the inside skate and takes the ice on its inside edge. Simultaneously, the inside leg drives sideways under the body toward the outside of the curve as it thrusts against the outside edge of the blade.

Deke—Fake.

Edge of the blade—The sharp part of each skate blade that cuts into the ice. There are two edges on each blade. The following abbreviations are used throughout the book to describe the edges used to perform skating maneuvers:

- RFI—Right foot skating forward on the inside edge
- RFO—Right foot skating forward on the outside edge
- RBI—Right foot skating backward on the inside edge
- RBO—Right foot skating backward on the outside edge
- LFI—Left foot skating forward on the inside edge
- LFO—Left foot skating forward on the outside edge
- LBI—Left foot skating backward on the inside edge
- LBO—Left foot skating backward on the outside edge

Flat of the blade—Both edges engage the ice simultaneously. The glide will be straight ahead.

Flexibility—The ability to move a muscle group through its full range of motion.

Free foot, hip, leg, shoulder, or side—Those parts of the body that correspond to the skate that is off the ice.

Full extension—The part of the stride where the knee of the gliding leg is well bent and the thrusting leg is locked and as far away from the body as it will stretch.

Gastrocnemius—The muscle in the back of the calf.

Gliding foot (skate)—The foot on which the full body weight is sustained while moving over the ice. Also known as the skating foot.

Gluteal muscles—The muscles of the buttocks.

Groin—The crease at the junction of the thigh with the trunk.

Groin muscles—Muscles of the groin area.

Hamstring muscles—The long muscles in the back of the upper leg.

Inside edges of the blades—The blade edges closer to the insides of the boots.

Inside foot (skate)—When one is skating a curve, the foot (skate) closer to the center of the circle or curve.

Inside shoulder—When one is skating a curve, the shoulder closer to the center of the curve.

Lacebite—A contusion, or bruising, of the tendons of the upper foot caused by excessive pressure on the tendons. The condition is very painful and can be caused by lacing the skates too tightly.

Lower body—The body from the hips down: hips, buttocks, legs, and feet.

Outside edges of the blades—The blade edges closer to the outsides of the boots.

Outside foot (skate)—When one is skating a curve, the foot (skate) closer to the outside of the curve.

Outside shoulder—When one is skating a curve, the shoulder closer to the outside of the curve.

Plyometrics—Movements or exercises involving recoil-bounding (coil-spring) actions.

Quadriceps (thigh muscles)—The muscles at the front of the upper leg.

Rock of the skate blade—The convex curvature of the blade.

Rockering the blade—Creating a specific convex curvature of the blade during the sharpening process.

Skating foot, hip, leg, shoulder, side—Those parts of the body that correspond to the skate that is engaged on the ice.

Thrusting foot (pushing foot)—The foot that pushes against the ice to propel the skater.

Toe of the blade—The extreme front of the inside or outside edge of the blade, including the curved portion, that provides the final push.

Torque—A turning or twisting force.

Transition—A change in direction of movement that does not necessarily involve a turn of the body.

Traveling on a curve or circle—Moving in a clockwise or counterclockwise direction.

Turn—Changing the body position from skating forward to skating backward, or from skating backward to skating forward, which may or may not involve a change in the direction of travel.

Upper body—The parts of the body from the waist up: waist, abdomen, chest, arms, shoulders, and head.

V or open turn—A two-step maneuver used to turn from forward to backward or from backward to forward with the feet in a "V"-like position prior to turning and changing feet.

references and recommended reading

Alter, M. 1990. *Sport Stretch*. Champaign, IL: Human Kinetics.

American Sport Education Program. (1996). *Coaching Youth Hockey*. Champaign, IL: Human Kinetics.

Blatherwick, J. 1986. *Team U.S.A. Year Round Training*. Colorado Springs, CO: Amateur Hockey Association of the United States.

Clifford, C., and Feezell, R., 1997. *Coaching for Character*. Champaign, IL: Human Kinetics.

Endestad, A., and Teaford, J. 1987. *Skating for Cross-Country Skiers*. Champaign, IL: Leisure Press.

Foeste, A. 1999. *Women's Ice Hockey Basics*. New York, NY: Sterling.

Holum, D. 1984. *The Complete Handbook of Speed Skating*. Hillside, N.J. : Enslow.

Powell, M., and Svensson, J. 1993. *In-Line Skating*. Champaign, IL: Human Kinetics.

Publow, B. 1999. *Speed on Skates*. Champaign, IL: Human Kinetics.

Siller, Greg. 1997. *Roller Hockey: Skills and Strategies for Winning on Wheels*. Indianapolis, IN: Masters Press.

Twist, P. 1997. *Complete Conditioning for Ice Hockey*. Champaign, IL: Human Kinetics.

Wenger, H. 1986. *Fitness: The Key to Hockey Success*. Victoria, British Columbia, Canada: British Columbia Amateur Hockey Association.

about the author

© Erik Hill

Internationally renowned power skating coach **Laura Stamm** has been coaching hockey players for 30 years and is considered the pioneer of modern power skating. The first woman ever to coach a major league professional hockey player, Stamm has shown the hockey world how important skating technique is to a player's success. She has worked with college and youth hockey players, U.S. Olympic team members, and professional players representing many National Hockey League (NHL) teams. Stamm has taught thousands of amateur and pro players, including many NHL stars, how to increase their speed, ability, and efficiency on the ice.

Stamm has taught the Los Angeles Kings, the New York Rangers, the New York Islanders, and the New Jersey Devils. Her Power Skating System has been employed by prestigious teams around the world.

A champion athlete in ice dancing and tennis, Stamm majored in physiology at Cornell University and went on to teach high school biology and physics. In 1971 she became a power skating coach at a summer hockey school directed by then-NHL stars Rod Gilbert and Brad Park. She went on to coach rookie New York Islander star Bob Nystrom. Her enormous success with him led to coaching assignments with other teams in the NHL and WHA (World Hockey Association).

Stamm currently conducts power skating clinics throughout the United States and Canada for players of all ages and abilities. She is the author of two successful earlier editions of this book, two other books, dozens of articles, and two instructional videos on power skating; she is also a noted speaker and TV personality. Stamm's other interests include dancing, backpacking, kayaking, photography, and music. She lives in Anchorage, Alaska.

Your one-stop hockey resource center!

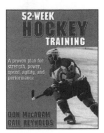

Approx 200 pages
0-7360-4204-0

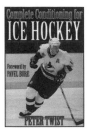

256 pages
0-87322-887-1

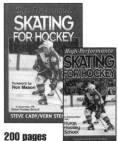

200 pages
53-minute videotape
0-7360-0094-1

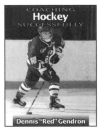

Approx 232 pages
0-88011-911-X

216 pages
0-88011-736-2

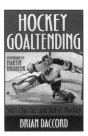

200 pages
0-88011-791-5

192 pages
0-87322-998-3

216 pages
0-7360-0004-6

For more information on
these and other hockey resources,
visit the Human Kinetics Web site at
www.humankinetics.com

To place your order, U.S. customers call

TOLL FREE 1-800-747-4457

Customers outside the U.S. should place orders using the appropriate
telephone number/address shown in the front of this book.

 **HUMAN KINETICS**
The Premier Publisher for Sports & Fitness
P.O. Box 5076, Champaign, IL 61825-5076